First published 2014 by Croft Publishing

Copyright © 2014 Rodney J. Croft

Rodney J. Croft has asserted his right
under the Copyright, Designs and Patents Act 1988
to be identified as the author of this work.

ISBN 978-1-50295-694-1

Also available in a Kindle ebook edition
ISBN 978-1-84396-331-8

Cover design by Alex Croft

Cover and event photographs reproduced
under licence from Topfoto and Getty Images. Other
photographs from the author's collection.

Photograph of Andrew Roberts
courtesy of Nancy Ellison

Photograph of Rodney J. Croft
courtesy of Hazel-Ann Croft

A CIP catalogue record for this
book is available from the British Library.

All rights reserved. No part of this
publication may be reproduced, stored in or
introduced into a retrieval system or
transmitted in any form or by
any means electronic, photomechanical,
photocopying, recording or otherwise
without the prior permission of the publisher.
Any person who does any unauthorized act
in relation to this publication may be liable to
criminal prosecution.

Pre-press production
www.ebookversions.com

*In memory of my parents,
Ronald and Joan Constance Croft,
and to my wife Hazel-Ann
and the Croft family.*

CHURCHILL'S FINAL FAREWELL

*The State and Private Funeral
of Sir Winston Churchill*

RODNEY J. CROFT

CROFT PUBLISHING

Contents

'Operation Hope Not'   i

Preface   1

Foreword
by Andrew Roberts   3

Introduction   7

Chapter 1
*State and Ceremonial Funerals
and 'Operation Hope Not'*   17

Chapter 2
Churchill and Death   39

Chapter 3
Lying-in-State   61

Chapter 4
*The Procession to
St Paul's Cathedral*   65

Chapter 5
The Service in St Paul's Cathedral   **79**

Chapter 6
*The Procession to Tower Pier
and on to Festival Pier and Waterloo*   **89**

Chapter 7
*The Train Journey from
Waterloo to Hanborough*   **107**

Chapter 8
*The Interment at
St Martin's Church, Bladon*   **117**

Chapter 9
Return to London   **123**

Conclusion   **125**

Epilogue   **127**

Appendix I – Churchill Graves   **133**
Appendix II –   **135**
Sources, Bibliography
Appendix III – Poems   **140**
Appendix IV – Tribute Events   **143**

Acknowledgements 145

About the author 153

Illustrations

The Duke of Norfolk, Ted Dexter, and Alec Bedser	9
Lying-in-State, Westminster Hall	62
Gun carriage leaving Westminster Hall	67
Gun carriage, Whitehall	69
Gun-carriage procession led by the Duke of Norfolk	73
Funeral service invitation	74
Funeral service ceremonial guide	74
Funeral service seating card	75
Order of Service at St Paul's	76
Arrival of coffin at St Paul's	77
The service in St Paul's	83
The Queen and Prince Philip leaving St Paul's	87
RAF flypast and the dockland tribute	99
Funeral train departs leaves Waterloo	101
Funeral train speeds to Hanborough	109
Winston and Clementine Churchill's grave at Bladon	119
Statue of Sir Winston Churchill in Woodford Green	125
Churchill at an RAAF ceremony in Croydon, 1948	129
Rodney J. Croft	153

'Operation Hope Not'

This is the first book ever published having as its sole subject the State and Private Funeral of Sir Winston Churchill, who died on January 24th 1965 – the same date his father, Lord Randolph who died on January 24th 1895.

The year 2015 marks the 70th anniversary of the end of World War Two, in which Churchill played such a pivotal and dynamic role. And it is also the 200th anniversary of the Battle of Waterloo and the 600th anniversary of the Battle of Agincourt.

The book covers all aspects of 'Operation Hope Not', the code name for the arrangements for Churchill's State Funeral and only made available to the public on January 31st 1995 under the 30-year official secrecy rule. The author had access to Archive papers at Arundel Castle, West Sussex; the Churchill Archives Centre at Churchill College Cambridge; the National Archives at Kew, Richmond, Surrey; and The College of Arms in London. He interviewed in 2013 the 11th Duke of Marlborough – who – as the Marquis of Blandford – greeted and then accompanied the mourners after the service at St. Paul's Cathedral on the funeral train to Hanborough; then on to St. Martin's

Church Bladon, where Churchill's burial took place.

The author also interviewed, in 2013, the Countess of Avon (Churchill's niece), who attended the funeral, and Mrs. Minnie Churchill, who attended Churchill's Lying-in-State and who is the mother of Churchill's living heir, Randolph Churchill – Winston Churchill's great grandson.

The book also covers aspects of State and Ceremonial funerals and gives details of Churchill's State and Private Funeral; the reasons why Waterloo Station not Paddington Station, was chosen as the departure point from London to Bladon in Oxfordshire, where Churchill lies, and the story of his interment there.

There are also particulars given of some rather special champagne served on the train with a personal message from Winston – stories that the 16th Duke of Norfolk, the Earl Marshall of England who was responsible for all the arrangements for 'Operation Hope Not' told his close friend, the great English bowler Alec Bedser. Their friendship had been forged during the M.C.C. tour of Australia and New Zealand in 1962-63, when the Duke was Manager and Alec Bedser the Assistant Manager of the M.C.C. Touring side. Sir Alec Bedser and his twin brother Eric subsequently became very firm friends of the author for over 35 years and Alec Bedser told the Duke's stories to the author.

*'I am ready to meet my Maker.
Whether my Maker is ready for the ordeal
of meeting me is another matter.'*

Winston Churchill on the occasion of his 75th birthday

'It wasn't a funeral, it was a Triumph!'

Lady Clementine Churchill: as said
to her daughter Mary, later Lady Soames, on retiring
in the evening after Winston Churchill's funeral,
January 30, 1965

Preface

January 30th 2015, marks the 50th anniversary of Sir Winston Churchill's State and Private Funeral, six days after his death at the age of 90 on January 24th 1965, the same day that 70 years before Sir Winston's Father, Lord Randolph had died in 1895 at the age of 45 and the date Sir Winston had quite amazingly prophesised as the date of his death, some years previously, as mentioned to his Assistant Private Secretary Jock Colville, one morning whilst shaving.

The year 2015 also marks the 70th anniversary of the end of World War Two, in which Churchill played such a colossal and crucial role; and 2015 is the 200th anniversary of The Battle of Waterloo and the 600th anniversary of The Battle of Agincourt.

This is the first book written with its sole subject the State and Private Funeral of Sir Winston Churchill. There is an extensive list of all references sourced from archives, books, contemporary journals, magazines, newspaper, and digital recordings – together with information obtained from private interviews, which has been used in the text.

This book tells for the first time, the full story of Churchill's final farewell, his State and Private Funeral on

January 30th 1965 and the events leading up to that momentous, moving, and totally unforgettable day.

Foreword
by Andrew Roberts

In January 1965 Britain was embarked on an era of liberal transformation of civil society under her prime minister Harold Wilson (whether for better or worse must be a question for debate for a long time to come). At that moment a towering figure from its history was laid to rest with all the splendour and reverence for which the country was famous. It is now fifty years since Sir Winston Churchill was interred at Bladon in Oxfordshire – close to his place of birth, Blenheim Palace. By popular vote he is the 'Greatest Briton' ever to have lived, which is a large claim in a history so rich in larger-than-life characters and a series of acute national crises over the centuries. I was only two years old at the time, though I envy my elder cousins who attended the event that day.

Rodney Croft has given us a fitting tribute to the national hero in this often intimate story of both his state and private funerals. This diligent author has had the enthusiastic support of the Churchill family and has interviewed many people who attended the funeral, both as mourners and as officials participating in or overseeing the event. It was, of course, planned with the attention to detail of a military operation, and was timed to the last minute.

It is fascinating to see how – as with Royal funerals – the planning began long before Churchill's death, and how the plans had to be adapted to changes in circumstance. Between his research in numerous archives and his personal contacts, Rodney Croft has become, sometimes by coincidence and sometimes at one or two removes, the repository of some intriguing stories, most of them in print here for the first time. Railway enthusiasts and bell ringers alike will be delighted with the scale of detail entered into.

To read the speeches given during the funeral is a signal reminder of the power of oratory. Both Dwight D. Eisenhower, for the United States of America, and Robert Menzies, for Australia and the Commonwealth, delivered moving thanks for the leadership qualities of Winston Churchill, both during the Second World War and in the post-war world. Yet it is still, however familiar they may be to us, the words of the man himself during life that continue to inspire us after all these years.

We are reminded of the colossal danger the world faced between 1939 and 1945, and how one man famously mobilised the English language and turned it into a weapon in the struggle for freedom and democracy. The fight against tyranny was long and hard, but it was necessary. Whenever we become exasperated with our politicians, we should remember that we live in a democracy, however imperfect, and we have never succumbed to tyranny, nor ever will. That will be largely due to the example of Winston Churchill.

Hardly a day passes without a mention of Churchill somewhere in the world's media. The Churchill Centre is a vibrant international organisation that seeks to conserve his memory and teach the democratic principles that he lived by to subsequent generations. He was a fully-rounded human being; he had his faults; but, besides his renowned 'bulldog spirit', he had the most wonderful sense of humour. The mischievous wit of Winston Churchill informed the planning of his own funeral and is an integral part of this delightful study of such a great event.

To paraphrase Winston's wife, Clemmie, speaking to her daughter, Mary, 'It was not a funeral, it was a triumph!'

Andrew Roberts's Masters and Commanders *was one of the most acclaimed, bestselling history books of 2008. His previous books include* Salisbury: Victorian Titan *(1999), which won the Wolfson History Prize and the James Stern Silver Pen Award for Non-Fiction, and* Hitler and Churchill: Secrets of Leadership *(2003), which coincided with a four-part BBC2 television history series. His latest book,* Napoleon the Great, *was published to acclaim in 2014. Andrew Roberts is one of Britain's most prominent journalists and broadcasters.* (Photograph courtesy of Nancy Ellison)

Introduction

The reasons I decided to write this book result from a long and circuitous, but nevertheless, interesting story covering some 67 years.

My initial introduction to Churchill was by my late Mother, Joan Constance Croft, who when I was a young child would say to me on my birthdays 'Happy Birthday and just remember, Rodney, you were born six weeks premature – just like Winston Churchill.' This became indelibly etched in my memory and as I began to learn more about this amazing man over many years, from this rather specially shared neonatal experience of premature birth, I developed both a keen and deeply felt affinity, together with an enormous admiration for the great Winston Churchill.

It is said that everyone who heard of President J. F. Kennedy's assassination can remember exactly where they were when the news was broken. I was in Hall at Selwyn College Cambridge having dinner; I can recall precisely on which bench I was sitting wearing my black *in statu pupillari* short gown, eating jugged hare. I cannot, like I suspect millions of others, remember where I was precisely when the death of Sir Winston Churchill was announced on January 24th 1965, no doubt owing to the immense media coverage preparing us for the news of his inevitable death after his final and ultimately fatal stroke on January 15th 1965. But what I, with I believe, millions of other people around the world can remember is precisely where I was when I watched Sir Winston's Funeral on BBC Television. Without doubt it was the most moving and momentous occasion we had ever witnessed or perhaps ever will.

In 1975 I was introduced to the famous cricketers the Bedser twins, Alec (Surrey and England) and Eric (Surrey), by my then Surgical Consultant Frank Henley, a General and Colo-Rectal Surgeon at Central Middlesex Hospital in London. Over the years the Bedser twins and I became very firm friends and I subsequently became their surgeon following Frank's retirement in the 1980s. During a visit to The Oval Committee Room at the kind invitation of the Bedsers, to watch a Test Match against Australia, Alec told me the story of when he was made Assistant Manager to the touring M.C.C. side to Australia and New Zealand in 1962-3. To the surprise of many in the cricketing establishment, the then 16th Duke of Norfolk, Bernard Marmaduke Fitzalan-Howard, had been appointed Manager of the M.C.C. Ashes and New Zealand touring side. Norfolk certainly knew a great deal about horses and although he loved the game of cricket, was not an accepted expert by the cricketing fraternity.

Moreover, Norfolk was not used to handling money; indeed whenever he came up to London from Arundel, Lavinia, the Duchess, would give her husband a purse containing the necessary money with a written note inside listing the price of the train ticket, the taxi fare from the station to the Duke's Club and other essential financial

The Duke of Norfolk, Ted Dexter, and Alec Bedser as they embark on the MCC tour of Australia and New Zealand in 1962-63.

requirements for the day. There is no way Norfolk could have handled the financial affairs of an M.C.C. tour; sharing gate monies, paying expenses and players, and neither did he know the grounds in Australia. Alec Bedser having toured a number of times to Australia playing for England, not only knew the Test Match game well, but also knew the grounds and was adept with financial matters, so he was the perfect choice to assist the Duke. During the tour they developed a very firm friendship which lasted for many years and subsequently involved frequent Bedser twins' visits to Arundel Castle and Ascot at the Duke's and Duchess' invitation.

The Duke left for Australia for the M.C.C. tour on

October 1st 1962 and returned to England for a short time on or around December 10th. The first Test at Brisbane, a six day, eight ball over match was from November 30th-December 5th 1962. The Duke again returned to England in early January 1963, returning to Australia on March 20th. In his absence, the Duke was replaced by Billy Griffiths the Secretary of the M.C.C.

It was thought Norfolk's departures were for emergency meetings concerning 'Operation Hope Not'. However these departures were planned before the Tour began (Arundel Castle Archives Ref: EM 3687/ 236, letter from Norfolk to Sir Norman Brook Cabinet Secretary 27th July 1962). Churchill had fractured his left hip in June 1962 requiring surgery and was hospitalised for two months. It was thought by some that he would not recover, which might have explained the Duke's planned returns to England.

In the letter outlining the timetable above, the Duke stated that everything (Churchill's funeral arrangements) was well prepared, and that it would only be the four days before the funeral that everyone would be very busy. The Duke also pointed out that everyone knew their jobs and could begin even if the Duke was not in England. (Arundel Castle Archives, Ref: EM 3678/236).Norfolk having returned in March stayed with the M.C.C. touring team until their return to England after the tour of New Zealand. At the end of the 1962-63 M.C.C. Tour, the Duke submitted his Manager's report which ends thus:

> I must end this report by referring to the Assistant Manager, Alec Bedser. No one could ever take on a tour such as that of Australia and New Zealand without an Assistant Manager but no one, in the future, will be as

lucky as I was unless they have Alec Bedser. Apart from his efficiency and hard work his devotion to the whole business was quite remarkable, and the success of the tour was very largely due to the tremendous friendship that he already has with so many of the officials connected with the cricket in the different States.

M.C.C. can never be better served than they were by him, and I end by expressing my grateful thanks to Alec who has become a real friend in every sense of the word.

Norfolk.

(Arundel Castle Archive, DB27; reproduced by the kind permission of His Grace The Duke of Norfolk.)

This provides irrefutable and compelling evidence of the strong friendship which had developed between The Duke and Alec Bedser. As an aside, the Duke was not at all so praiseworthy of Fred Trueman, England's fast bowler on the M.C.C. tour who despite being England's second highest wicket taker (20 wickets at an average of 26.05 runs; Fred Titmus took 21 wickets), displayed behaviour and lack of team spirit was not at all what The Duke expected.

Norfolk was The Earl Marshal of England responsible for organising State occasions including Churchill's State Funeral. After Churchill's Funeral, Norfolk told Alec Bedser why Waterloo not Paddington was chosen as the departing railway station from London to Hanborough and then to St. Martin's Church in Bladon near Blenheim Palace in Oxfordshire after The State Funeral at St. Paul's. He also told Alec about a message on the funeral train accompanying some special Champagne for the mourners; but more of this later.

I now move forward to 2008 when my wife and I were holidaying on the wonderful and beautiful northern atoll of Kanuhura in the Maldives, reached excitingly by Otter seaplane from the capital Male. One morning, sitting on the beach, I was reading a book entitled *Winston and Jack* by the historical authors Celia and John Lee, the story of the two Churchill brothers and outlining why Winston's brother Jack had to some extent been airbrushed out of history.

In the book the authors allude to Winston's premature birth at Blenheim Palace and the extraordinary claim by a biographer in 2006 that Jennie Churchill had provoked her emergency delivery. She had gone into labour whilst walking on a game shoot at Blenheim, and had elaborated on the deception by not having baby clothes or a specialist doctor to hand to conceal she was pregnant before her marriage. Others suggested that such a healthy baby could not be premature and that Churchill's parents had consummated their relationship before marriage.

The neonatal mortality rates for premature babies in Victorian times were known to be high but these figures were significantly skewed by the majority of premature babies being born to impoverished and working-class mothers. There were no separate statistics for premature babies born into the aristocracy or wealthy families. Jennie was healthy and well-nourished and the aftercare of an infant was excellent. Indeed, The Duchess of Marlborough had quickly arranged for a wet nurse from Woodstock to be present while Jennie was in labour so Winston was fed immediately after he was born.

Churchill was delivered after an eight hour labour in the downstairs cloakroom in Blenheim Palace where there was a bed with a brass bedstead from its use as quarters for the chaplain to the first Duke. Churchill was delivered by a local doctor Frederic Taylor. In *Winston and Jack*, gestation (duration of pregnancy) was calculated as 36 instead of 40 weeks. Whereas pregnancy is frequently referred to as nine months, in reality it is 40 weeks from the date of the first day of the last menstrual period (LMP), so Winston was more than likely to have been four and a half to six weeks premature rather than the three weeks which Celia and John Lee had calculated.

Having read these facts and having done some mental arithmetic, I arose from my sun bed, under the palm covered wide conical sunshade outside our beach villa, which overlooked the calm lagoon and beyond to the reef, clutching Celia and John's book and walked along the soft white sand to the small library near the reception with its palm leafed roof where there was a computer where I wished to confirm my thoughts.

I searched a calendar for 1874, the year of Randolph and Jennie's marriage on April 15 1874 and Winston's birth on November 30 1874. Assuming on the balance of probabilities, Winston's Mother Jennie had a regular menstrual cycle and also taking into account the wishes of a bride regarding the timing of her honeymoon in relation to this, one could more than reasonably assume that Jennie's LMP was in late March or early April 1874 and that Winston's full-term birth date would have been during the first two weeks of January. Based on these calculations Winston was conceived in wedlock and was four and a half to six weeks premature. After all my mother could not possibly be wrong. She would never have misled me.

Also, Winston's lower jaw bone (mandible) was fractured at birth; he was not a breech delivery which might have given rise to this injury by the *accoucheur* assisting delivery by placing two fingers in the baby's mouth and pulling firmly down on the lower jaw and once the lower part of the face presented, then lifting upwards to assist delivery of the crown of the baby's head. This very rare complication of a normal delivery could well have been the result of force on a premature child's mandible which would be underdeveloped and therefore weaker. Therefore, it is certainly more than likely than Winston was conceived in wedlock, thereby strongly challenging any theory to the contrary. He was therefore, certainly in my view, a honeymoon baby and not for the first time.

I corresponded by email with Celia Lee from the Maldives, from my little palm leaf covered roofed computer room and gave my opinion for which she was extremely grateful. I was then asked by her and husband John to contribute as a medical expert to Celia and John Lee's subsequent book, *The Churchills* published in 2010.

My views had become even more relevant following further biographical accusations of Churchill being conceived out of wedlock in 2008. I was subsequently asked to present my research on Winston's premature birth to the Woodford and Epping Branch of The Churchill Centre.

My friendship with John and Celia has grown considerably and one evening at a Churchill Centre meeting in Chigwell, Essex, I told Celia the Norfolk story Sir Alec Bedser had related to me in the 1980s regarding the reason for the choice of Waterloo not Paddington and the message with the special Champagne from Winston. Celia insisted I should write a letter to *Finest Hour* the quarterly publication of The Churchill Centre outlining Norfolk's story. Fortunately as it now turns out, the Editor, Richard Langworth, declined to publish the story as it could not be corroborated; I had every reason to believe The Duke and my great friend Alec Bedser, so I then set on a course to verify the story.

My journey took me to The archives at Arundel Castle, The Churchill Archives Centre, Churchill College, Cambridge, The National Archives at Kew and The Archives at The College of Arms in London.

I have been most fortunate to meet and interview Churchill's great-grandson, Randolph (Churchill's surviving heir, born two days before Winston's death) and his mother Mrs Minnie Churchill who was in Westminster Hospital for twelve weeks before Randolph's birth having threatened to miscarry. Mrs. Minnie Churchill was taken to the Lying-in-State in Westminster Hall in a wheelchair and was unable to attend the funeral as she was still then hospitalised.

I have also interviewed His Grace the 11th Duke of Marlborough in 2013 at Blenheim Palace in his private study. As the Marquis of Blandford in 1965, His Grace greeted the mourners onto Churchill's funeral train after the service at St. Paul's Cathedral. I also interviewed in 2013 the Countess of Avon – the niece of Churchill and the wife of Anthony Eden, who both attended Churchill's funeral.

So all of this, together with Norfolk's story related to me by Sir Alec Bedser and my rejected letter, has metamorphosed into this book. It has been a most interesting and adventurous journey, which I have thoroughly relished. I sincerely hope you will find reading it as interesting as I have found researching and writing it.

RODNEY J. CROFT
Buckhurst Hill

November 2014

Chapter 1

State and Ceremonial Funerals – 'Operation Hope Not'

In the United Kingdom, a State funeral refers to that of a Monarch, the last of which was in 1952 for King George VI. It consists of the body being taken by a horse-drawn gun carriage from the private resting place to Westminster Hall for a period of Lying-in-State for three days. Westminster Hall was first used for this purpose in 1898 for the past Liberal Prime Minister, William Gladstone's State funeral. The coffin draped with the Royal Standard and the Imperial State Crown upon it, is placed on a tall catafalque. During the Lying-in-State when members of the public are allowed to pay their last respects, each corner of the catafalque is guarded by members of the Sovereign's bodyguard and the Household Division. Following the Lying-in-State, the body is carried on the gun carriage hauled by sailors of the Royal Navy for the procession to Paddington Station, thence on to Windsor where the funeral service and burial takes place in St. George's Chapel, Windsor Castle. (Queen Victoria was buried at Frogmore

House in the Home Park at Windsor). During the journey to Paddington, a large procession accompanies the monarch consisting of military personnel, members of the Royal Household, and close to the coffin, the dead monarch's personal staff and servants. Equerries serve as pallbearers who walk alongside the coffin which is escorted by the Sovereign's bodyguards, the Gentlemen at Arms and the Yeomen of the Guard. The Royal Family follow the coffin as do Commonwealth and foreign dignitaries.

State funerals have been held for commoners in the past and include: Sir Isaac Newton, (1727); the English physicist and mathematician who discovered gravity; The Viscount Nelson (1806), who famously won but died at the Battle of Trafalgar; The Duke of Wellington (1852), who triumphantly defeated Napoleon at Waterloo; William Gladstone (1898), Liberal Prime Minister; and Earl Haig (1928), Field Marshall of The British Expeditionary Force in World War One.

Those granted Ceremonial funerals include: The Earl Mountbatten of Burma (1979), Diana, Princess of Wales (1997), Queen Elizabeth The Queen Mother (2002) and The Baroness Thatcher (2013).

State funerals for those outside the Royal Family largely follow the format above except the site of the funeral service and burial is different. Whereas State funerals are overseen by the Earl Marshall of England, the Duke of Norfolk, a Great Officer of State together with his officers, the Heralds, Ceremonial funerals are organised by the Lord Chamberlain, an officer of the Royal Household. For a Commoner a State funeral requires a Motion in The House of Commons.

A Ceremonial funeral is in essence the same, as that

granted to Baroness Thatcher, except the gun carriage is horse-drawn, not pulled by naval ratings. The exception to this was the ceremonial funeral of The Earl Mountbatten of Burma where naval ratings hauled the gun carriage in respect for his long service in the Royal Navy. The history of the use of naval ratings dates back to Queen Victoria's funeral in 1901 which was the first time a gun carriage had been used to convey the monarch. The train from Paddington to Windsor was delayed and everyone was kept waiting including the horses harnessed to the gun carriage for one and a half hours. It was a bitterly cold day with light snow falling. The mounted troops gave their mounts some gentle circling movements to keep them relaxed, but the four horse team from X Battery, Royal Horse Artillery stood harnessed in their traces for all this time. When the train finally arrived, the coffin was placed on the gun carriage and on the order to advance the rear horses reared up without moving off which was followed by similar equine consternation in the lead horses. There were present 100 naval ratings, sent for street lining duties at Windsor Station and Prince Louis of Battenburg moved over to the naval guard commander, Lieutenant Algernon Boyle and instructed him to order his men to ground their arms and to stand by to haul the gun carriage. Within five minutes, the horses had been unharnessed and moved away. The Naval Ratings made drag ropes from the harness traces and communication cords from the train and were then ordered to slow march.

The Army version of events given by Lieutenant M.L. Goldie commanding X Battery was that as the order was given to advance, an eye hole on a splinter bar broke and in the ensuing confusion he was disallowed from giving the emergency action drill order. In any event the Navy won the day much to the glee of an Admiral who was present. Since that day the Royal Navy has maintained the honour of hauling the gun carriage.

The gun carriage's gun was made by Vickers Son and Maxim in 1896 and stored at the Royal Arsenal Woolwich. It never fired a shot in anger and the gun carriage was converted in 1899 by the Royal Carriage Department Woolwich, where it was fitted with a bier in order to carry a coffin, but its normal fittings of a hand spike, spade and spring case were left in situ. The gun carriage was issued to X Battery Royal Horse Artillery in 1901. Subsequent to Queen Victoria's funeral, King George V presented the carriage to H.M.S. "Excellent" in Whale Island, the Royal Navy's Gunnery School in Portsmouth harbour in Hampshire, founded in 1830. It had in fact been kept in the naval stores since 1901 as Captain Adam R.N. did not want to give it back to the Royal Artillery who understandably never made the request! The sailor's legend at Whale Island was that every time the King reported ill, the gun carriage was whipped out and given a polish up!

Her Majesty The Queen made her wish known in the 1950s after her Coronation in 1953 that Winston Churchill should be afforded the State funeral normally reserved for a Monarch. On Churchill's death, The Queen would issue her command for a State funeral. (Churchill Archives Centre Ref: CHUR 1/137 No. 1, letter to Montague Browne from David Stephens Jan 27 1958.) On March 13th 1957, Earl Rocksavage, 'Rock', the 5th Earl of Cholmondley and the Lord Great Chamberlain wrote to the Duke of Norfolk stating that Churchill would lie in State in Westminster

Hall. (College of Arms Archives Ref: The funeral of Sir Winston Churchill, Vol. II, 26/2/57). So the plans were well afoot in the late 1950's.

The Duke of Norfolk who also holds the Title of Earl Marshall of England, a position held by the Dukes of Norfolk since 1668, is responsible for arranging all State occasions including State funerals. It was therefore the responsibility of Bernard Marmaduke Fitzalan-Howard, the then 16th Duke of Norfolk, to make all the necessary arrangements for Churchill's funeral. The extensive plan for the funeral was secretly referred to as "Operation Hope Not", but entitled, *The State funeral of The Right Honourable Sir Winston Leonard Spencer-Churchill KG OM CH*. (copies of the purple backed volume can be seen at: Arundel Castle Archives, West Sussex, (Ref: EM3690), Churchill Archives Centre, Churchill College, Cambridge (Ref: SEAG/24) College of Arms, London, (Ref: Funeral Papers of Sir Winston Churchill Vol. II) and The National Archives, Kew (Ref: CM/209). The book was first released to public view on January 31 1995 in compliance with the 30 year secrecy ruling. The use of 'Hope Not' in the early 1950's turned out to be very apt as Churchill survived another 15 years. The final edition consisted of 115 pages with extensive maps numbered over 300. The heading inside the book was listed as *Special District Order by Major-General E.J.B. Nelson D.S.O., M.V.O., O.B.E., M.C., General Officer commanding London District and Major-General commanding House-hold Brigade*. The final edition was dated 24 January 1965.The plans were immensely detailed, even down to where troops would be able to obtain a bun and a hot drink. The troops involved were to total 575

Officers and 6508 Other Ranks, which, for a commoner, were numbers last seen for The Duke of Wellington's State funeral in 1852, on whose funeral Churchill's was based. All mustering, assembly and dispersal points were clearly outlined with timings down to seconds. The assembly points for the Processional Troops were: Horse Guards Parade, Wellington Barracks and Millbank. The troops lining the processional route mustered at Whitehall Place, Waterloo Bridge, Temple Place, Blackfriars, and Southwark Street. Every assembly was timed to the minute. It outlined in detail all involved in the procession and the distribution of troops lining the processional route. Breakfast was to be provided in the concentration areas, lunch was in the troops' haversacks and the evening meal in the concentration areas or barracks. It really was a masterpiece of logistics and organisation.

There were also elaborate plans drawn up by the Metropolitan Police. The book has an appropriately blue coloured cover with the same title as the 'Operation Hope Not' book and consists of 47 pages of extremely detailed information including lists of senior officers and personnel on duty, the timings of the parades the dress to be worn, the route The Queen and Royalty would take from Buckingham Palace and details of the Funeral Procession. There were details of the formation and keeping of the Police lines with barriers, corridors and cordons. Full details of all communications were listed, including traffic arrangements and route control. There were even full details of refreshment arrangements, citing precisely where canteens were to be placed, wet weather contingencies, overnight patrols and First Aid facilities. The order for wet weather was that the funeral would go ahead, irrespective of the weather, with the exception of very severe fog, which would cause movement to become unworkable. Like 'Operation Hope Not', it seems that nothing was left to chance and every possible, minute detail was recorded.

There was also a document, *Operation Order No 801*, concerning traffic arrangements, which was 59 pages long and printed on 14 and a half inch paper, a size normally reserved for instructions for royal occasions. It contains all conceivable information as how traffic was to be controlled, how traffic lights were to be turned off in the closed off streets, the list and times that bridges over the Thames were to be closed and then re-opened and when the roads were to re-open. There was then an appendix with a list of 527 officers with service numbers and rank and where precisely they were to be placed and their duties. There were 282 officers on night patrol before the funeral day, a total of 580 on daytime patrol and points. There was also an appendix listing the different windscreen labels which were distributed. Finally there was a full timetable of Police events from 2am on the morning of the funeral until the train departed Waterloo at 1.25 pm.

Sergeant David Morehen of the Metropolitan Police was very much involved in the production of these plans as he typed them out. When they were proof read there was only one typo, a lower case 's' was upside down, but the typesetter's fault, not his! Quite amazing and is a great tribute to Sergeant Morehen's typing skills. His story begins when he took a shorthand and typing course whilst he was still a lowly Constable as it was a way of escaping from Cannon Row Police Station in the 1950's. The other routes of escape were to take a motorcycle course or get married, about which he admits he knew nothing. He went to evening classes at Westminster Technical College and qualified. He thereafter applied for a clerical position in the Public Order Branch at New Scotland Yard, the Headquarters of the Metropolitan Police and was successful in obtaining the post. He was then involved in the organisation of State occasions such as Trooping the Colour, the State opening of Parliament, occasional State visits of Kings and Queens, Presidents and overseas leaders. He remembers being involved also with the wedding of Princess Alexandra – a daughter of Prince George And Princess Marina, the 1st Duke and Duchess of Kent. During this time, he was living very near to his senior officer, Chief Superintendent Bill Best in New Malden and in 1959 was invited to the Superintendent's home one Sunday afternoon and instructed to bring his shorthand notebook. He was then warned that what he was about to be asked to do was 'Secret' and although he was to work on the project in the office for some months he was not to divulge any details of his work outside the office. The superintendent then began to dictate the police plans for 'Operation Hope Not' which became File 14/59/46, one of those 14 and a half inch files reserved for Royalty and very special occasions which clearly this was. Bill Best was always going to meetings at the Lord Chamberlain's Office and having dealings with Garter King of Arms at the College of Arms and at the headquarters of the Household Brigade. He would then dictate his notes of the meetings to officer Morehen. That draft was developed over the ensuing years during which time David Morehen was promoted to Sergeant. He was in his office when he heard of Churchill's death and knew instinctively what he had to do to set the 'wheels in motion'. He rang his wife and asked her to send round his toothbrush and pyjamas and then with his colleagues worked throughout the next week, day and night, until the funeral itself. Such was the dedication of all those concerned with 'Operation Hope Not'.

By April 1958 it was clear, following the Lying-in-State at Westminster Hall, the procession would proceed to St. Paul's and thereafter to Tower Pier. The final destination was then Chartwell via Greenwich, South East London, on the south bank of the River Thames, (Option C) but in June of 1959 this was changed to Gravesend, Kent, on the south side of The Thames Estuary, (Option B), as depicted on the Ordinance Survey map in Arundel Castle Archives, (Ref: EM 3686 No. 63.)

In December 1958 the categories and allotments of seats for those to be invited to the Funeral were drawn up. Based on an availability at St. Paul's of 2,500 the categories were: the Sovereign and members of the Churchill family; The Lord Mayor and family; members of the House of Lords; Foreign Office and Privy Councillors; Ministers; Members of Parliament; Great Officers of State; judges and legal officers; Knights of The Garter; aldermen and representatives of the City of London including Livery Companies; members of the Civil Service; towns; constituencies; Officers and staff of the House of Commons; members of the Royal Navy, Army and R.A.F.; mayors and local government; Colonial Office; Commonwealth Relations Office; Scottish Office; Northern Ireland Office; London County Council; Merchant Navy; civil aviation; industry; the press; and miscellaneous – including representatives of the main organisations with which Churchill was connected. (College of Arms Ref: Funeral of Sir Winston Churchill Vol.II, 11/12/58).

Churchill's original wish as stated in all the copies of his wills prior to December 31st 1959 was to be cremated, (Churchill Archives Centre, Ref: CHUR 1/138 No. 150). Information from the Cremation Society and a card with a policy number was found in Churchill's papers, (Churchill Archives Centre, Ref: CHUR 1/138 p. 101) and his ashes were to buried in the grounds of Chartwell House in the croquet lawn with its small white painted wooden croquet hut, near the pet cemetery where his prized pet brown poodles Rufus I and Rufus II lie. Churchill's cat Jock, given to Churchill and named by him after his Assistant Private Secretary Jock Colville was curled up on Churchill's bed when he died. Jock, the cat, outlived him by nine years and is also buried in the pet cemetery near the top terrace. Now at Chartwell is Jock VI, an extremely handsome marmalade cat with his red collar. The original bequest to the National Trust stipulated the cat must be marmalade with four white paws and a white bib. What sets Jock VI apart from the usual Jock model, which meets the bequest stipulation, is his amazing golden eyes and his most distinguished milk moustache.

The plans for the Lying-in-State in Westminster Hall were therefore drawn up, which were to be followed by the gun carriage transfer of Churchill to St. Paul's Cathedral rather than Westminster Abbey, due to the former's nearer proximity to Tower Pier, for the journey by launch downstream on the River Thames to Gravesend, a two hour sail and thereon by motor hearse to Chartwell, a journey of 25 miles and precisely timed at 73 minutes. In 1959, it was originally decided to use the steam yacht " St.

Katharine" but as she was in dock for repairs the Trinity House yacht "Patricia" was earmarked as the vessel to be used for the Thames journey. (Arundel Castle Archives Ref:EM 3686, No.5, letter 26/1/59). The last person to be carried by boat on the Thames in a State funeral was Viscount Lord Nelson in 1806, when he was carried from Greenwich to St. Paul's. In the Archives at Arundel Castle is a one inch to the mile Ordinance Survey map with the route from Gravesend to Chartwell marked in a strong black line. The title on the map's cover is 'Operation Hope Not'. (Arundel Castle Archives, Ref:EM 3686 No. 63). Instructions were that as the coffin passed under Tower Bridge, in The Pool of London, the proceedings would thereafter be private.

However, towards the end of 1959 it became known that Churchill had visited St.Martin's Church in Bladon, Oxfordshire, in view of Blenheim Palace where he was born and where in the Churchyard other members of the Churchill family are buried including his father Randolph Churchill and his mother Jennie. It is said that Churchill tapped an empty plot with his walking cane and said 'This is my place here'. This change of mind by Churchill resulted in a letter from the Cabinet Secretary Sir Norman Brook to The Duke of Norfolk in December 1959 stating that he thought that this would mean considerable changes in his plans! (Arundel Castle Archives, Ref: EM 3686, No. 96). The 10th Duke of Marlborough had conveyed in March 1958 that Churchill's final resting place would be the little church which could be seen from the steps of Blenheim about two miles away through a gap in the trees, St. Martin's Bladon. So maybe Churchill's visit to Bladon was in 1958, unless the Duke made an accurate prophesy, based on where Churchill's ancestors lay in the family plot, of what Churchill's later and final wish would be. Churchill was very fond of Blenheim and said that is was where he made the two most important decisions of his life: to be born and to be married. The fact that his ancestors were buried at Bladon and its close proximity to Blenheim must surely have been the decisive factors in his final decision.

Churchill's will of December 31 1959, therefore changed his wish to be buried in the Churchyard of Bladon near Woodstock (Churchill Archives Centre, Ref: CHUR/138 p.150). His will of 20th October 1961 confirmed these wishes. His Executors were Lady Churchill, Mary Soames and John ('Jock') Colville. (Churchill Archives Centre, Ref: WCHL 5/3).

The nearest station to the village of Bladon in Oxfordshire is Hanborough for Blenheim, on the Western Railway Worcester line from Paddington and the journey by road from St. Paul's to Paddington is only four and a half miles via Fleet Street, The Strand, Constitution Hill, Park Lane, Bayswater Road and thence to Paddington. Even in 1958, in correspondence to Sir Norman Brook it was mentioned that if Blenheim should be the ultimate place of interment there was everything to be said for a procession to Paddington.

The story told to Sir Alec Bedser by the Duke of Norfolk was that when Churchill had decided to be buried at Bladon, the V.I.P guest list was being discussed between the two of them. When Norfolk came to Charles De Gaulle, The President of France and Leader of the Free French during World War Two, Winston insisted that if De Gaulle outlived him he did not wish him to attend his funeral. Churchill still remembered the difficult times he had encountered with De Gaulle during the war years despite subsequent *rapprochement,* at least in public. Roy Jenkins, the Labour then Social Democrat politician, in his book, *Churchill* (Macmillan, 2001), alludes to the violent relations, mostly down rather than up, Churchill had experienced with De Gaulle for four and a half years from May 1940. Churchill once referred to De Gaulle as looking like 'a female llama who has just been surprised in her bath.'! (*The Wicked Wit of Winston Churchill* Dominique Enright, Michael O'Mara Books Ltd., 2011). Shortly after the sinking of the French Fleet in Oran in 1940 owing to the failure of the French Navy handing over their ships to the Royal Navy, De Gaulle was invited to have lunch with Winston and Clementine in No. 10, Downing Street. Clearly in view of recent events the atmosphere must have been somewhat tense to say the least. The subject turned to the future of the remainder of the French fleet based in Toulon, then part of Vichy France, which the French ultimately scuttled before German forces arrived in November 1942 to seize the fleet. Clementine expressed the hope that they would continue the fight against the Axis powers with us. De Gaulle replied that he felt the French fleet would prefer to turn their guns on the British! Clementine who spoke very good French admonished the General for his remark which she correctly felt ill-became an ally or a guest in this country, perhaps not to mention, a guest in her dining room. Churchill tried to intervene by saying De Gaulle should excuse his wife as she did not speak fluent French which she did, but Clementine was quite adamant saying that there were things a woman could say which a man could not and she was sticking to her guns. After this altercation, the General clearly upset apologised profusely and the next day sent Clementine a large basket of flowers.

Max Hastings in his book *Finest Years*, Harper Press 2010, describes how Churchill in 1941 was 'sick to death' with De Gaulle's petulance and discourtesy. Also Hastings refers to a plane crash which Randolph Churchill, Winston's son survived and while recuperating met his Father and heard a strong denunciation of De Gaulle. In 1945 Churchill refused to allow De Gaulle to attend the Yalta Conference with Stalin and Roosevelt on the premise France could not masquerade as a great power for the purposes of war. Churchill once remarked that De Gaulle 'thinks he is Clemanceau having dropped Joan of Arc for the time being'. (Mary Soames Ed., *Winston and Clementine: The Personal Letters of the Churchills*, Boston: Houghton Mifflin, 1999, p.475). Lord Moran Churchill's personal physician also noted that De Gaulle seemed to positively go out of his way to be difficult and that he frequently got on Churchill's nerves. (*Churchill The Struggle for Survival 1940/65*, p.87, Lord Moran, Constable and Company, 1966). In 1940 De Gaulle blamed the advance of the German army in France on lack of British army support and yet 400,000 troops had been sent to France and France's capitulation almost resulted in the loss of the British Expeditionary Force. The Royal Air Force had shot down 400 enemy planes over France but to the annoyance of the British, the French released German pilots some of whom were then involved in the Blitz bombing of some of our towns and cities. The final straw was perhaps when it was known in 1941 that De Gaulle had remarked that he did not care whether or not Britain won the war as what really mattered was that France was saved. He also blamed the Americans for problems initially encountered in the invasion of North Africa, 'Operation Torch'. Churchill's fury led him to seriously consider replacing De Gaulle with a triumvirate of General Giraud, the hero of World War One, ex-Prime Minister Camille Chautemps and Alexandre Leger, who had been the head of the French Foreign Office. However, the wise counsel of the then Foreign Secretary, Anthony Eden – that the French saw De Gaulle as the leader of the French Resistance and should remain – prevailed. On the eve of 'Operation Overlord', the Allied plan for the invasion of France, Churchill showed De Gaulle the plans who then asked to send the details to his committee in Algiers. Churchill was obviously furious and adamantly refused the request as the telegraph could well have been intercepted and compromised the whole operation. De Gaulle stormed out of the meeting.

The UK first applied for membership of the European Economic Community in 1961 when Harold Macmillan was Conservative Prime Minister and which was then negotiated by Edward Heath as Lord Privy Seal. Then in 1963 came the famous 'Non' rebuttal from President De Gaulle. Our second application, then to the European Community was in 1967 which was finally successful, but not until 1973 when Ted Heath was Prime Minister. So from 1959-64 when Churchill's funeral plans were being compiled and finalised, there was no possibility whatsoever, the UK political establishment would have wished to annoy the French in any way. Interestingly, when Churchill was in the Woolavington Wing at The Middlesex Hospital, in London after his hip operation in

1962, there was a wonderful cartoon by Low who then worked for *The Guardian* entitled, "The Battle of Middlesex Hospital", showing Winston in bed, wearing his pyjamas and a nightcap and smoking a cigar. He is spraying a soda syphon over Montague Browne, his private secretary cowering at the end of the bed, who was urgently on the phone to Lord Beaverbrook the newspaper tycoon and owner of *The Daily Express*. On Winston's bed is a book with the title, *Common Market*.

In Paris in 1958, De Gaulle had awarded Churchill the Ordre de la Liberation and a year later in Westminster Hall when De Gaulle gave his tribute to 'Le Grand Churchill', Churchill was in tears and those present felt they were witnessing the reconciliation between these two great but sometimes pretty impossible men. However, it seems Churchill understandably never forgot the petulant times during the war years.

Norfolk apparently pleaded with Churchill that in the interests of *Entente Cordiale* and the UK's wish to join the European Union that De Gaulle should be invited. Eventually Churchill acquiesced but on the one condition that his funeral train would leave from Waterloo not Paddington. Waterloo was on the Southern Railway line whereas Hanborough was on the Western Railway line from Paddington Station. However, there was a disused spur at Reading which linked the Southern Railway to the Western Railway. It was known in railway circles that Churchill knew of the spur and he was therefore in the knowledge this journey by rail to Hanborough from Waterloo was perfectly possible. The Churchill's knew about railways; Randolph, Churchill's father had shares in the Southern Railway and the London Midland and

Scottish Railway and there is no doubt his sons Winston and Jack also took a keen interest in railways.

On December 22 1959 The Earl Marshall and Mr. Montague Browne, Churchill's Private Secretary, went to see Sir Norman Brook, the then Cabinet Secretary. The Earl Marshall stated that following discussions with the Police and London District there would be 'difficulties' in arranging for a procession to go as far as Paddington (Churchill's father's old constituency) from St. Paul's Cathedral, a mere four and a half miles. His alternative suggestion was that the procession should go to Tower Pier, and from there on to Festival Pier and Waterloo. The Earl Marshall was then invited to arrange for plans to proceed on this basis. (Churchill Archives Centre, Ref; CHUR/147, p. 50, Note for Record December 22, 1959). Churchill therefore had his wish granted to have Waterloo front of stage on his final farewell day for all to see, including the French President. In 1960 it was suggested to Norfolk that Churchill's body after the service at St. Paul's could be conveyed by river to Westminster Pier on the north bank of the Thames, thereby fulfilling a river journey together with R.A.F. flypast and then on to Paddington a mere three and a half miles away, but this idea was quashed in favour of Winston's wish for Waterloo. (College of Arms Archives, Ref:The Funeral of Sir Winston Churchill, Vol. II, letter 10/4/58).

Waterloo was known as the sailors's station, as it was the main railway route to the large naval port, Portsmouth, Hampshire and was also the funeral station. In 1854, there was a crisis in London as the capital no had longer any significant number of cemetery plots left in the capital. The Necropolis Railway was therefore founded, with its station part of the Waterloo Terminus and its line going to the huge new cemetery at Brockwood in Surrey. Colloquially, the trains were referred to as 'The Stiffs' Express'. The trains could carry 48 bodies at any one time and the coffins could travel first, second, or third class. At the station there were facilities for storing coffins, waiting rooms for mourners and facilities for religious services, none of which was required on the day of Churchill's funeral. Waterloo station began to expand in the beginning of the twentieth century so the Necropolis terminus was moved to Westminster Bridge Road in 1902. Following a bombing raid in April 1941, it was finally closed. Waterloo Station was therefore historically seen as the funeral station but there really was no functional necessity for Churchill's train to leave from Waterloo; it could have been awaiting the cortège procession at Paddington Station. Churchill's impish sense of humour was well known and indeed alluded to by Anthony Eden in his tribute to Churchill after his death. Harold Macmillan, Conservative Prime Minister, in his tribute commented that Churchill's obstinacy was exhausting, but his puckish sense of humour and his tremendous sense of fun and his quick alternation between grave and gay, was a joy to witness. Norfolk's story of why Winston insisted on Waterloo is just so 'Winston'.

Following the decision to use Waterloo Station as the departure point for Bladon, the spur between the Southern Railway and Western Railway lines was maintained in order to be ready for use at any time in the future.

It was also agreed that if it seemed Churchill were to die within 24 hours, Mr. Montague Browne would send

The Earl Marshall and Sir Norman Brook a telegram with the single word 'imminent'. The arrangements for returning Churchill's body to England if he died overseas were also confirmed. A telegram was sent to overseas Embassies to make it clear that foreign countries, 'in particular France', should be asked that any ceremonial should be only at the point of departure such as the airport or seaport from where the Royal Navy or Royal Air Force would convey the body to England and thereon by rail to Victoria station, irrespective of where the death occurred, except if in London. It was also decided that the AA and RAC should be asked to appeal to motorists not to bring their cars into the City on the day of the funeral.

Lady Churchill in 1960 asked the then Rector of St. Martin's Church Bladon to conduct the interment service; there was to be no service within the Church and the Rector H.C. Woods was to meet the cortège and the mourners at the Churchyard Lych-gate before proceeding the 25 yards or so to the graveside where he would recite the short committal from the Prayer Book beginning 'Man is born of a woman' to 'they rest from their labours' and as was written in the 1928 version finishing with 'Now unto the King eternal…' (Churchill Archives Centre Ref: CHUR/1/137 No. 104)

In 1964, Lady Churchill aware that there would be a period of Lying-in-State and also aware of Churchill's wish to be cremated, expressed the opinion that it might be better for Sir Winston's body to be cremated before the Lying-in-State. (Churchill Archives Centre Ref: CHUR 1/138 No.101).The alternative would mean the necessity to embalm the body which was distasteful to the family. The Earl Marshall and Garter King of Arms at the College of Arms were advised to seek the advice of the Archbishop of Canterbury who felt that if the family would accept the idea of embalming it would avoid the possible risks of public dissatisfaction. The Archbishop was wary of the psychological uneasiness which would prevail if a great procession and public ceremony of a Lying-in-State was centred on the coffin containing only Churchill's ashes not his body. The Archbishop thought the family might have a misconception of embalming which was a very simple matter and might therefore wish to discuss this with their medical advisors. (Churchill Archives Centre Ref: CHUR 1/138 p.64). There is no record as to whether this discussion ever took place. However the decision was made to embalm Churchill's body after his death to enable it to be in his English oak lead-lined coffin for the duration of the Lying-in-State and his State funeral. Keynons, the London undertakers, took care of these matters.

By 1960 the orders were clear that after the service at St. Paul's the coffin was to be taken to Tower Pier and that MV "Havengore" would then proceed to convey the coffin to Festival Pier and then by motor hearse to Waterloo Station. In the 3rd edition of 'Operation Hope Not', dated February 10 1960, precise timings are listed: 12.50pm launch departs Tower Pier, 1.05pm arrives Festival Pier, no doubt to coincide with the high tide so that the deck of "Havengore" was as level as possible with the piers to facilitate the transfers of the coffin.

During the next few years there were further editions of 'Operation Hope Not' with various modifications but the plan for the procession from New Palace Yard to St. Paul's for the service and thereafter to Tower Pier for the river journey to Festival Pier and Waterloo, then Hanborough and Bladon remained extant. The date of the last edition was January 24 1965, the date of Churchill's death.

Chapter 2

Churchill and Death

Churchill was not particularly religious; he was not a regular churchgoer but was pleased to attend church services as weddings, christenings and funerals. He once said of death and life thereafter, 'Some kind of cool blackness. Of course, I admit I may be wrong. It is conceivable that I might be reborn as a Chinese Coolie. In such a case, I should lodge a protest.' (*The Wicked Wit of Winston Churchill,* Dominique Enright, Michael O'Mara Books 2011). He also said that he loved life but did not fear death. Perhaps like many of us, he would have agreed with the words of the late Dudley Moore – that great actor, comedian, and musician – whose comment on all this was that he had not remembered his birth and sincerely hoped he would not remember his death.

During Churchill's life he had experienced a number of near misses with death; in 1866, when aged 11, whilst at boarding school he developed serious pneumonia and was considered close to death before he finally recovered after his temperature had reached 104 degrees fahrenheit.

While on holiday in Bournemouth in 1893 he was trying to escape from his brother Jack and his cousin during a holiday chase. They finally cornered Winston on a bridge who in order to escape then decided to leap off the bridge on to an adjacent tree. Unfortunately, he lost his grip and fell 30 feet, to the ground below resulting in a period of unconsciousness for three days, due to a significant head injury. He also suffered a damaged kidney and a fracture of the shaft of his left femur (thigh bone), which was later seen as an old healed fracture on an X-ray when he fractured his left hip in Monaco in 1962. In 1922 Churchill underwent an emergency appendicectomy for a gangrenous appendix which in that era carried a significant mortality rate. (Dr. John H. Mather, personal communication, *Churchill The Supreme Survivor*, p.52-56, A.W. Beasley, 2013, Mercer Books).

He first came under fire on his 21st birthday while in Cuba; this was the first of about 50 such occasions during his life. In 1895, he had gone as a Lieutenant in the 4th Queen's Own Hussars with a fellow officer to witness the Spanish fighting the Cuban guerrillas having been commissioned to write about the conflict for *The Daily Graphic*. In 1897 Churchill was in the Malakand Field Force on the North West Frontier and was mentioned in dispatches after 'making himself useful at a critical moment'.

He was then later involved in the last major cavalry charge in British Military history with the 21st Lancers at the Battle of Omdurman in September 1898 against the Dervishes. The very last cavalry lance-on-lance engagement, which lasted just 15 minutes, was in 1914 at Montcel-Fretoy in the Battle of the Marne involving the

9th Lancers whose commander was a previous amateur jockey who had won the Grand National; the Germans were routed. After this, the machinegun ruled.

At Omdurman a section of the 21st Lancers right wing where Churchill was riding, suddenly came upon and were outnumbered by Dervishes, concealed in a khor, a dried watercourse or shallow ravine and it was certainly a potentially lethal situation which necessitated a hasty retreat. Due to an old right shoulder injury, (he had previously first dislocated his right shoulder in 1898 when going ashore in Bombay in a skiff, when he had reached up and grasped a ring secured in the sea wall in a heavy swell and the skiff suddenly fell thereby wrenching and dislocating his shoulder), Churchill's sword remained sheathed and he instead carried a Mauser pistol which he had purchased in London and which with some accurate firing no doubt aided his escape and saved his life. After this original dislocation, there were recurrent episodes and whenever playing polo Churchill carrying his stick in his right hand, would wear a leather strap around his chest which had a loop holding his right arm close to his chest in order to prevent a further recurrent dislocation.

There were 310 officers and men in the Omdurman charge during which 21 had been killed and 50 wounded in the khor engagement, against only a total of 28 killed in the whole battle. So it really was a highly dangerous encounter and his accident in Bombay harbour resulting in his original shoulder dislocation may well at Omdurman saved his life. Churchill may well have lost his life during the engagement with the Boers in South Africa when the armoured train on which he was travelling was ambushed resulting in his capture prior to his incarceration as a prisoner of war in Pretoria. Then, within three weeks, followed his renowned escape to Mozambique and triumphant return to England via Lorenzo Marques having spent some days hidden from the Boers in a Scottish miner's mine shaft during which time he understandably became quite claustrophobic.

In World War One, when serving on the Western Front a piece of shrapnel shattered an Orilux trench torch Churchill was carrying which resulted in major damage to the strong metal side of the top of the torch which might well have caused serious limb injury or death if the shrapnel had landed a few inches away from where it struck. The lamp can be seen in the exhibition at Chartwell House, Westerham, Kent.

Also a flying accident might have proved more serious: Churchill was having a flying lesson in 1919 and came into land. He made a misjudgement resulting in a crash landing and suffered some minor scratches and bruises but the crash did render the instructor unconscious, albeit not for a protracted period.

During peacetime, he might have come close to death when in New York in 1931. Forgetting that cars drive there on the right he stepped out from the pavement on the corner of Fifth Avenue and 72nd Street straight into the path of a New York Taxi driven by Mario Constasino from Yonkers. He suffered painful injuries to his right leg and thigh and cuts and bruises but this episode might well have been more serious. 'It was all my fault,' Churchill later said. He spent a week as an in-patient at Lennox Hill Hospital and experienced severe paraesthesiae (pins and needles) in his arms and legs together with some temporary weakness of all four limbs demonstrating he had incurred a significant cervical spine (neck) injury. Thereafter, he carried a scar on his forehead, seen on subsequent photographs including the famous portrait taken by Yousef Karsh the Canadian photographer in 1941 in Downing Street, when Karsch snatched Churchill's cigar from his mouth and instantly took his picture. (*Churchill The Supreme Survivor*, p.64, A.W. Beasley, 2013, Mercer Books)

Churchill had also witnessed death close to in members of his family. His father Randolph died in 1895 from a serious neurological disorder at the age of 45 years when Churchill was 20 years old. Also his mother Jennie died in 1921 when she was 67 and Churchill was 46 years old; it was the same year that Clementine's brother Bill committed suicide in Paris. Jennie had been getting ready for dinner in the upstairs room of a friend's house when dinner was called. She quickly put on a new pair of high-heeled shoes for which the maid had not had time to sandpaper the soles. Descending the stairs from her room, she slipped and fell down the stairs resulting in a serious fracture of her leg. Sadly the fractured area subsequently turned gangrenous necessitating an above knee amputation. Some days after the operation she felt her dressing become very wet; she had clearly developed a secondary haemorrhage due to infection eroding a major blood vessel, likely to have been the femoral vein, the main vein above knee level and she succumbed to this massive bleed. Also Churchill's third daughter and fourth child, Marigold, born in November 1918, at the age of two years and nine months developed a cold-like illness; there was an epidemic of Spanish flu at the time, but whatever her initial illness, this then developed into what seems to have been a septicaemia, (a blood infection due to bacteria), probably due to the bacterium streptococcus, the bacteria responsible for such illnesses as tonsillitis, scarlet fever and cellulitis, an infection of the soft tissues and skin. This was before the days of antibiotics and Marigold died shortly afterwards on August 23 1921. She was buried in Kensal Green Cemetery in 1947. There is a lovely photograph of Marigold on Clementine's bedroom desk at Chartwell and next to it is the last known photograph taken of Winston.

Churchill also lost his brother Jack who died of heart disease; he had developed a cardiac aneurysm a bulging of part of the heart muscle. They had been fellow soldiers who both served together in the Boer War. Winston was present at Jack's bedside with much shedding of tears when his brother died in 1947 aged 67. He felt his brother's death very keenly. Winston was not well enough to attend Jack's funeral at Bladon during the bitter winter but later attended his brother's memorial service in London. Churchill also lost another daughter Diana who after a long period of mental illness died from an overdose of barbiturates in 1963 at the age of 54. There were also three other deaths in the Churchill family during his lifetime of more distant relatives.

While in Washington in 1941, Churchill suffered a heart attack (myocardial infarction) which demonstrates he had established atherosclerosis (hardening of the arteries) at the age of 67 years. (*Churchill The Struggle for Survival 1940/65*, p.16, Lord Moran, 1966, Constable and Company). He also suffered a bout of pneumonia around this time, no doubt exacerbated by his cigar smoking.

Churchill first began smoking cigarettes at age 15

while at Harrow, for which his mother admonished him. When at Sandhurst he changed to cigars and his love of Havana cigars began during his visit to Cuba in 1895 to witness the action of the Spanish against the Cuban guerrillas. Whilst there he smoked La Aroma de Cuba cigars and then in later years, his favourite, Romeo Y Juliet. He would smoke a cigar down to a couple of inches then give the stubs to his gardener at Chartwell to smoke in his pipe. He would also smoke in bed which resulted certainly on one occasion, alluded to by his butler, in a burnt hole in the sheet from dropped ash. Figures of the numbers of cigars smoked in a day are perhaps exaggerated but number six to eight. (*Churchill's Cigar*, Stephen McGinty, 2007, Macmillan) So he smoked cigars for 70 years and if he averaged six a day, this would total over this long period of time, somewhere in the region of 150, 000. Like most cigar smokers, he did not inhale, a fact he alluded to in World War Two when visiting a parachute factory where he took out a cigar from his pocket and the Fire Officer yelled that he shouldn't smoke to which Churchill told him not to worry as he did not inhale!

Over many years he was given a number of gifts of cigars by the Cubans. A particular one was a handsome, tall, inlaid wooden humidor containing 3,000 cigars from the Cuban National Tobacco Commission. This lovely humidor now stands to the left of Churchill's easel in The Studio at Chartwell, with its doors open and on its shelves are numerous tubes of Churchill's oil paints. Some of the cigars were tested for poison in 1941 by the British Secret Service, M.I.5.; a few Churchill smoked but as Churchill did not wish for anyone to whom he gave the cigars to be poisoned, they were destroyed. Nevertheless, the humidor made a wonderful oil paint repository.

In 1949 whilst in Monte Carlo, Churchill suffered his first stroke at the age of 75, (*Churchill The Struggle for Survival 1940/65*, p.333, Lord Moran, 1966, Constable and Company); he felt a cramp-like feeling in his right arm and leg which by the next morning affected his right hand, making writing difficult but the neurological deficit was short lasting. He then suffered between this time and his fatal stroke in January 1965 eight more strokes, some minor, some more serious. He also had a gangrenous area on a finger tip and also a period of reduction in arterial blood flow to a leg, so he was an arteriopath, a patient with significant and generalised arterial disease. He also had bouts of atrial fibrillation, an irregular heart beat and it was noted by the eminent neurologist Lord Brain in 1955 that it was difficult to palpate (feel) the carotid pulses, the main arteries supplying the brain, in the neck. So Churchill's strokes could have been a combination of embolic disease from his heart (clots breaking off from within the heart and travelling to other parts of the arterial circulation) or from heavily diseased carotid arteries in his neck or disease of his intra-cerebral arteries (the arteries within the brain) or a combination of all three.

A stroke or cerebrovascular accident can be due to a clot (thrombus) developing within a cerebral artery or travelling from the heart or from the carotid (from the Greek word 'to stupefy') or vertebral arteries in the neck up into the brain. Approximately 87% of strokes are thrombotic and 13% are haemorrhagic due to a bleed from a burst artery in the brain. Haemorrhagic strokes are associated with uncontrolled hypertension (high blood pressure) and thrombotic stokes are associated with a number of high risk factors for cardiac and cerebrovascular thrombotic disease. A thrombus emanating from the heart, an embolus, is usually associated with an irregular pulse particularly in atrial fibrillation, a condition where the right atrium, a chamber of the heart receiving oxygenated blood back from the lungs beats irregularly and not in a coordinated way. As a result thrombi (clots) can form in the small appendage of the left atrium which can then become dislodged and having been ejected from the left ventricle can then travel to anywhere in the arterial circulation causing a blockage of an artery which in the brain can result in a stroke.

In the blood stream there are red blood cells and white blood cells. There are also platelets which resemble microscopic matchsticks which for a clot to form need to aggregate, rather like turning a full matchbox upside down on a table, and if they then adhere form a scaffold for the circulating blood in the immediate vicinity to form a clot. Such platelet aggregations can form on the surface of a diseased artery such as the carotid. The aggregation can then grow like a stalagmite or stalactite, fracture off and ascend into the cerebral circulation causing mini-strokes (transient ischaemic attacks) or more serious strokes.

The human brain, like all primates, has a protection mechanism in that the four arteries supplying the brain, the two carotid arteries in the front of the neck and the two vertebral arteries at the back of the neck running up the cervical spine, all communicate with each other inside the skull through an arterial roundabout, the Circle of Willis, first described by an English physician, Thomas Willis (1621-1675). This can enable one of the four major arteries supplying the brain, such as a carotid artery, to become occluded (blocked) which would result in a major stroke in approximately 30% of cases as the three remaining arteries communicating via Willis' arterial roundabout can maintain adequate cerebral circulation. The poor gerbil for example does not have a circle of Willis, so if a gerbil's single carotid artery is ligated the result is a 100% major stroke; hence for many years the gerbil was used as the animal model in stroke research.

The risk factors for thrombotic cardiac and cerebrovascular disease are: smoking, excess alcohol intake which can cause platelet aggregation, high cholesterol, diabetes, atrial fibrillation, obesity and generalised atherosclerosis (hardening of the arteries). These are risks which with treatment and life style changes can now be controlled. The uncontrollable risks are: age, gender (more common in males), family history and history of previous stroke.

In 1949, Churchill was 75, so age was a risk factor, as was his gender. At this point he had not had a previous stroke and there was no family history of strokes. Churchill certainly smoked although not inhaling, he drank more than moderate amounts of alcohol; his nurse for a time, State Registered Nurse (S.R.N.) Angela Nicholls, said in interview in January 2014 that there was always champagne and brandy around. Angela Nicholls trained as a state-registered Nurse at Leeds General Infirmary qualifying in 1961 and worked at Hospital Paddington for a time after this. She then joined an agency, the Society of Chartered Nurses. In 1963 she was recruited as one of a team of nurses looking after Churchill, whom she first met at Hyde Park Gate in July 1963. Subsequently, while in Jersey when working in a café as a holiday job, she received a telegram from Miss Pew, the Matron at The Middlesex Hospital, London, requesting that she join Churchill in Monte Carlo on Onassis' yacht "Christina", which was sailing to the Greek Islands. She recalls the excitement of flying on a BEA flight to Nice and then on to Monte Carlo and then the happy memories of looking after Churchill as a member of the nursing team during the cruise. She remembers a photo of Churchill with three nurses in their bikinis and Randolph, Churchill's son, in swimming trunks. Thereafter, she spent some time at Chartwell but was in the United States when Churchill died.

We do not know what Churchill's cholesterol levels might have been, but there was no history of diabetes. He enjoyed a good diet and was overweight; his height was 5' 6' and his weight was, on admission to Lennox Hospital after his accident in New York in 1922, 13 stone (182lbs., 82.7kgs.). In subsequent years he looked heavier and his Body Mass Index would have been in the obese zone. There is certainly evidence that he suffered bouts of atrial fibrillation but this does not appear to have been for significantly long or continuous duration. There was a time during World War Two whilst in Carthage in North Africa that he had a rapid pulse, possibly atrial fibrillation, which resulted in an urgent call to Tunis for digitalis, a drug which helps to slow excessively fast and irregular heartbeats.

Churchill suffered a further stroke in 1953 affecting his left arm and leg. The right hand side of the brain controls the left hand side of the body and vice-versa, so now Churchill had suffered strokes affecting both sides of his brain; the left side in 1949 and the right in 1953. He then suffered two further strokes in 1955, one on June 2, again affecting his right hand and leg with the weakness lasting longer than on the first occasion. His pulse at this time was rapid, 120 per minute and irregular so he was probably suffering from atrial fibrillation then. On June 22 he had a recurrence of his stroke symptoms. At the end of 1955 during one of Churchill's glum moments it is recorded that Churchill had said to Lord Moran that he was waiting around for death but that it would not come. He also expressed the view that he did not expect to live for ever, but he wanted to know beforehand when his end was nigh. (*Churchill The Fight For Survival 1940/65*, p.659, Lord Moran, 1966, Constable and Company).

The ancient Egyptians used medicines made from willow and other salicylate rich plants and Hippocrates in the 4th century B.C. discovered that extracts from willow bark were efficacious in treating patients with painful ailments and fevers. It was then used by Galen in the first century A.D. In 1853 Charles Gerhardt produced acetylsalicylic acid for the first time and in 1897 Bayer in Germany, developed less irritating forms of the compound and then in 1899 had given the drug the name aspirin which lives on to this day. From 1924 Aspergum, a chewing gum containing aspirin was available in the United States and widely used as an analgesic (painkiller). The derivation of the word 'aspirin' comes from 'ASA', acetyl salicylic acid, acetylspirsaure in German. Spirsaure is the name for the meadowsweet plant spirea ulmaria from which salicylic acid could be derived. 'A' was taken from the acetylation, 'spir' from spirsaure and the 'in' was added for ease of pronunciation.

In 1950 a family practitioner, Lawrence Craven working in Glendale Memorial Hospital in California noted that children who had undergone removal of their tonsils (tonsillectomy) and also after tooth extraction and who were given Aspergum containing aspirin, for post-operative pain tended to bleed more after their operations compared to those who did not receive aspirin. This finding was published in a letter written by Craven to the *Annals of Western Medicine and Surgery*. Dr. Craven then gave aspirin to 400 of his patients who were aged 40-65 and over the next two years none experienced a major cardiac event. He wrote an article in the *Mississippi Medical Journal* in 1953 recording his findings, but they were not accepted by the medical establishment as he did not include a control group in his study so was not a truly scientific controlled trial. He expanded his study and gave regular aspirin to 8,000 40- to 65-year-olds. A year before his death, he recorded in his report of 1957 that not a single patient had died from a thrombosis. His letter and his articles gathered dust in a library archive until one day in the mid-1960s it was rediscovered and aspirin research began again in earnest. It was the found that the reason for Dr. Craven's observations was that aspirin, acetyl salicylic acid, was a powerful anti-platelet aggregator thereby preventing the formation of thrombi (clots). In fact a 75mg tablet of mini-aspirin taken by mouth has this effect within two hours and the effect of this single dose can last 10 days. Hence its rightful place now as a prophylactic (preventative) measure to prevent deep vein thrombosis (DVT) during long journeys such as long aircraft flights in conjunction with the wearing of lightweight graduated compression stockings or flight socks which improve the speed of venous return from the lower limbs, also assisting in the prevention of a DVT. However despite Craven's work and observations and the extensive research in the 1960s aspirin was not regularly used as anti-platelet therapy until the 1980's long after Churchill's death. Anticoagulants such as warfarin in Britain (licensed in 1954) and named Coumadin in the United States were not routinely used particularly to treat the embolic complications of atrial fibrillation until twenty five years or so after Churchill's death, although General Eisenhower having given up smoking 80 cigarettes a day in 1949, had been prescribed Coumadin after a heart attack in 1955; treatment which in Britain, was certainly way ahead of its time.

What really is quite amazing is that Churchill with all his risk factors and without the benefit of regular aspirin dosage or even warfarin survived another 15 years after his initial stroke, before his fatal stroke on January 15 1965. However, Churchill was known to have Disprin (soluble aspirin) first introduced in November 1948 to alleviate aspirin's gastric side effects) amongst his medicines, (*Churchill The Fight For Survival 1940/65*, p.688, Lord Moran, 1966, Constable and Company), but there is no record of him being a regular daily taker of the drug. Disprin contains 300 mgs of aspirin, so if Churchill was taking one or two tablets of Disprin at a time for headaches or pain from his arthritis, even every ten days or so, he would have unknowingly been having some intermittent anti-platelet therapy for some years – so this might well be the explanation of his quite remarkable fifteen-year survival to the age of 90, from his original stroke in 1949.

In June 1962 whilst in Monaco, Churchill fell and fractured his left hip; he was admitted to the Princess Grace Hospital in Monaco under the care of Professor Chatelin, the Head Surgeon, but and was then transferred by R.A.F. Comet back to England and then to the Woolavington Wing of The Middlesex Hospital in London where he underwent surgery performed by Sir Herbert Seddon and Mr. Philip 'Pip' Newman. 'Pip' Newman was a great orthopaedic surgeon who taught me orthopaedics as a clinical student at The Middlesex Hospital in the 1960s having come down from Cambridge having read Basic Sciences. He had been awarded the Military Cross for outstanding surgical services under enemy fire on the beaches of Dunkirk.

The anaesthetists were Dr. Peter Dinnick and Dr. Derek Cope both of whom taught me anaesthetics during my student days. Peter Dinnick gave my wife Hazel her epidural injection to ease her labour before giving birth to our first son, Alexander, at The Middlesex Hospital in 1974.

Churchill's pre-operative X-ray demonstrated a fractured neck of his left femur, (the bony stem from the shaft of the thigh bone to the ball of the ball and socket joint of the hip joint) and on the X-ray was also demonstrated the old healed fracture of the shaft of his femur dating from the previous injury when he fell from the tree in 1893.

On finally leaving the Woolavington Wing after two months, Churchill gave Seddon an antique silver handled basket made in 1797 and a box of 50 cigars. Newman received a silver salver and a box of cigars. Joyce Belding the Night Superintendent received a photograph of Churchill and also some cigars. (Churchill Archives Centre, Ref: CHUR 1/62 Nos. 3-6, 93, 83/84, 105, 113, 144)

Clementine Churchill said that Winston 'died' when he finally left the House of Commons on July 27 1964. He had previously left Number 10 for the last time on April 6

1955. Certainly after his hip fracture in 1962 Churchill's medical condition slowly declined until his fatal stroke and death in January 1965.

When Churchill suffered his ultimately fatal stroke on January 15 1965 whilst at his London home in 28, Hyde Park Gate, Lord Moran his personal physician would come out on to the steps of the house, to issue daily and later more frequent bulletins. Churchill's son, Randolph said at the time that his father took so long to die with Moran giving out all those bulletins over ten days. Indeed, there was a cartoon in one of the newspapers of Winston announcing the demise of Lord Moran! With the world's media giving Churchill's condition their full attention we were all being prepared for the sad eventuality which finally came on Sunday January 24 1965 shortly after 8am. He had been in a coma for some time and the last words he had uttered to his son-in-law Christopher Soames were, 'I'm bored with it all'. Churchill was surrounded by members of his family: Lady Churchill, their daughters, Mary (who was staying with her mother) and Sarah, Randolph, Churchill's son and his grandson Winston who had all been summoned by the nurse early in the morning. Grandson Winston said that they could all see that the end was nigh. Churchill was deeply unconscious and his breathing became very slow, 'and then he breathed no more'. His cat Jock lay on his bed and there were flowers and candles in his room. Lord Moran had arrived at Hyde Park Gate at 7.18am. He first informed The Queen and the Prime Minister Harold Wilson of Churchill's death and then at 8.35am his announcement 'Shortly after 8am, Sir Winston died at his home' was read to the 30 members of the Press standing in the rain by a member of the Press Association.

The Queen sent the following message to Lady Churchill:

> The whole world is the poorer by the loss of his many-sided genius while the survival of this country and the sister nations of the Commonwealth, in the face of the greatest danger that has ever threatened them, will be a perpetual memorial to his leadership, his vision and his indomitable courage.

Harold Wilson, the Prime Minister, wrote:

> Sir Winston will be mourned all over the world by all who owe so much to him. He is now at peace after a life in which he created history and which will be remembered as long as history is read.

These messages of condolences to Lady Churchill from Her Majesty The Queen and Harold Wilson were instantly transmitted around the globe and were published in the *New York Times* on January 25 1965. Their sentiments were echoed in later years by President Obama's words on the death of Nelson Mandela when he said, 'He belonged to us, now he belongs to the ages.' Certainly true of Churchill too.

President Lyndon Johnson was aroused from his sickbed in the Bethesda Naval Hospital and was informed of Churchill's death. The following statement was issued later in the morning:

> When there was darkness in the world and hope was low in the hearts of men, a generous providence gave us

Winston Churchill.

As long as men tell of that time of terrible danger and of the men who won the victory, the name of Churchill will live.

Let us give thanks that we knew him. With our grief let there be gratitude for a life so fully lived, for services so splendid, and for the joy he gave by the joy he took in all he did.

The people of the United States – his cousins and his fellow citizens – will pray with his British countrymen for God's eternal blessing on this man, and for the comfort to his family.

He is history's child, and what he said and what he did will never die.

(*The Times*, January 25 1965 page 8.)

The President issued an executive order requiring all flags to be flown at half-staff from all Federal buildings at home and all embassies and ships abroad until the interment. This was an unprecedented honour which according to The White House was the first time such a symbol of respect had been afforded a foreigner who was not a Head of State. Messages of condolence flowed in from leaders all around the world including a letter from General De Gaulle to The Queen and also to Lady Churchill. De Gaulle wrote to Lady Churchill:

> We take part from the bottom of our hearts, my wife and I, in the profound bereavement which has stricken you, your family, and at the same time, England and all men of good will in the entire world.
>
> In France, the death of Sir Winston Churchill is felt especially with much chagrin.

> For myself, I see disappear in the person of so great a man, my wartime companion and my friend. I beg you to accept, madame, my most respectful homage.

(*The Times*, Monday January 25 page 8.)

There were tributes published in *The Times* on January 25 1965 from Canada, Australia, India, Germany, Russia, Ghana, statements from Tel Aviv, Oslo, Athens, Beirut, Tokyo, Madrid, Rome, Stockholm, Geneva, Katmandu, Copenhagen and Kuala Lumpur. There were 46 books of Condolence subsequently received from countries around the World. At St. Paul's soon to be the site of Churchill's funeral service 'Great Tom' the State bell was tolled which usually only rang for the death of a monarch. Frank Hall the verger at St. Martin's, Bladon, on hearing the news went to the Church Tower to begin tolling the bell. Nicholas Soames, the son of Christopher Soams and Mary, (Churchill's daughter) was 16 years of age at Eton and his Housemaster came to tell him the sad news.

In the village of Westerham in Kent near Churchill's country home at Chartwell, a peal of muffled church bells were rung by the same bell ringers who had rung the joyous bells to announce during WWII that the threat of German invasion had passed. On the BBC radio the strains of Beethoven's 5th Symphony were played with the well recognised beginning of the Morse code rhythm of dot-dot-dot-dash, of 'V' for Victory, Churchill's famous hand signal. *The Times* broke with its then traditional custom of printing only the classified advertisements on page one where there was a tribute to Churchill. The Classifieds were moved to page three, the first time since World War

One. In the evening, the lights of Piccadilly Circus in Central London with the famous statue of Eros were switched off. Flags around the world were placed at half-mast including all Royal Naval ships including those at sea away from our isle and also on the Lightships protecting our shoals. At Lloyds, the world famous insurance market, the Lutine Bell rang once at noon – a traditional signal that a ship had been lost. At Salway Hill, Woodford Green in East London where Churchill had served as M.P., for the whole duration of the constituency from 1949-1964, when the boundary was then changed to Woodford and Wanstead, schoolchildren placed white chrysanthemums around his bronze statue, which had been sculpted by David Mc Fall in 1959 and unveiled by Field Marshall Viscount Montgomery in the presence of Churchill.

'Operation Hope Not' now swung into action; rehearsals began at 2am in the morning. Sergeant Morehen remembers seeing a gun carriage rehearsal in the early morning fog, an eerie experience which still lives with him. These rehearsals were led by Lieutenant Anthony Mather who alludes to nails and iron bars being placed in the coffin to match the weight of the coffin on the funeral day and which had been checked on a weighbridge.

The timings for 'Operation Hope Not' were as follows:

8.45am the doors of St. Paul's Cathedral open

9.40am. The Representatives of France, The United States of America and the Union of Soviet Socialist Republics arrive at St. Paul's.

9.45am The Cortège leaves New Palace Yard,

Westminster Hall

9.50am The Aldermen and High Officers arrive at St. Paul's.

9.55am The Members of The Royal Family, not being Royal Highnesses will arrive at St. Paul's

10.00am The doors of St. Paul's are closed to the public.

10.04am The Speaker arrives at St. Paul's 10.05am The Lord Chancellor arrives at St. Paul's.

10.13am The Foreign Heads of State and Royal Representatives arrive at St. Paul's.

10.15am The Heads of State and Royal representatives of Foreign Heads of State arrive at St. Paul's

10.23am Queen Elizabeth The Queen Mother and other members of the Royal Family arrive at St. Paul's.

10.25am The Lord Mayor of London arrives at St. Paul's

10.30am The head of The Coffin Procession reaches St. Paul's.

10.35am Her Majesty The Queen and His Royal Highness The Duke of Edinburgh and His Royal Highness The Prince of Wales arrive at St. Paul's.

10.45 am The Coffin arrives at St. Paul's.

10.49am The Earl Marshall's Procession enters St. Paul's and The Coffin is borne up the Nave

11.00am The Service begins.

11.30am The Service ends.

11.50 am The Coffin leaves St. Paul's.

12.25 pm The Coffin arrives at Tower Hill.

12.50pm Launch leaves Tower Pier for Festival Pier.

12.52 pm The Royal Air Force Fly-past.

1.05 pm The river Cortège arrives at Festival Pier.

1.20 pm The motor Cortège arrives at Waterloo Station.
1.25 pm The Special Train leaves Waterloo.

Everything was planned just like a full military exercise, down to the last minute and in some cases seconds.

Chapter 3

Lying-in-State

Westminster Hall used for the Lying-in-State was built by William Rufus in 1097 and was later altered by King Richard II in 1397. It was used for the trials of Sir William Wallace, Sir Thomas More, Guy Fawkes, The Earl of Strafford, King Charles I, The Scottish Jacobite Peers and William Hastings. It was used for Gladstone's Lying-in-State in 1898, King Edward VII in 1910, George V in 1936, George VI in 1952, and Queen Mary in 1953. (College of Arms Archives, Ref: The Funeral of Sir Winston Churchill, Vol. IV p.227).

A catafalque was built, measuring 40 feet long, 17 feet wide and 7 feet high.

It was covered with black velvet with a light yellow carpet over the pedestal. The floor of the cavernous hall frequently reverberated with the echoes of politicians scurrying footsteps and so was covered with a beige carpet to muffle the sound of people's slow foot treads filing past. The coffin was covered with the Union Flag upon which was placed the most prestigious honour bestowed upon

*Churchill's coffin at the
Lying-in-State in Westminster Hall.*

Churchill, the Insignia of the Most Noble Order of the Garter, with Collar, Star and Garter. There were no flowers but there were six large candlesticks with candles around the catafalque. One at each corner and the other two halfway along the catafalque.

There were five watch officers, one placed at each corner of the catafalque and one on the steps overlooking the catafalque all with heads bowed, their hands resting on their unsheathed swords. The duration of each watch was 20 minutes when the watch was changed. Early on the first day, the watch was taken over by Admiral of the Fleet, The Earl Mountbatten of Burma and the three Defence

Chiefs of Staff of the Royal Navy, Army and Royal Air Force: Admiral Sir David Luce, Sir Richard Hull and Sir Charles Elsworthy. This was in the tradition of the Vigil of the Princes for a monarch's Lying-in-State when Princes would complete a guard watch for their dead monarch.

The Lying-in-State was from Wednesday January 27 1965 to 6am on January 30. During this three and a half day period, Westminster Hall was open 23 hours a day and closed just for one hour for cleaning and vacuuming the carpets. Mary Soames, Churchill's daughter noted at the time the mass of people with their sombre dignity was like a river slowly flowing to honour him.

There were different entrances for visitors: Royalty via the East Door, V.I.P.s and Members of the House of Commons, the Crypt Door, Peers, St. Stephen's Hall and South Steps and the general public, St. Stephen's Porch and South Steps. On Her Majesty's command flags on all public buildings were to fly at half-mast until sunset on 30 January.

Mrs. Minnie Churchill – who gave birth to her son Randolph, Churchill's great Grandson, two days before Churchill's death – had been confined to bed in Westminster Hospital for twelve weeks, not even allowed to place a foot on the floor, owing to a threatened miscarriage. During my interview with her, she recalled being taken from her bed in Westminster Hospital to the Lying-in-State in a wheelchair. She recalled also the vast queues of people waiting to pay their respects and entering the somewhat dark Westminster Hall with its rather eerie cavernous sounds and the muffled footsteps slowly shuffling by the catafalque with not a single word spoken.

Sergeant David Morehen who had been very involved

in the drawing up of the Metropolitan Police plans for the funeral remembers 'jumping the queue', on strict instructions, to pay his respects to Churchill.

Over the period of three days, the queue reached three miles in length, stretching over Lambeth Bridge, and 4,000 people slowly filed past Churchill's body every hour; the final total of those who paid their last respects was 321,360.

Chapter 4

The Procession to St Paul's Cathedral

The procession to St. Paul's Cathedral and then on to Tower Pier with the escorts and the troops lining the streets of London involved 7, 000 military personnel which was equivalent to the number used for The Duke of Wellington's funeral in 1852. The Order of Procession was:

1. Metropolitan Mounted Police
2. Two Bands of the R.A.F.

Detachments of:

3. Battle of Britain Air Crews
4. R.A.F.
5. 4/5 (Cinque Ports) Battalion The Royal Sussex Regiment (T.A.)
6. 4/5 Battalion The Essex Regiment (T.A.)
7. 299th Field Regiment R.A. (T.A.) (Royal Buckingham Yeomanry, Queen's Own Oxfordshire Hussars and Berkshire)

8. Honourable Artillery Company (T.A.)
9. Royal Military Academy, Sandhurst
10. Two Bands of Her Majesty's Foot Guards
11 The Welsh Guards
12. The Irish Guards
13. The Scots Guards
14. The Coldstream Guards
15. The Grenadier Guards
16. Two Bands of the Royal Marines
17. The Royal Marine Forces Volunteer Reserve
18. The Royal Marines
19. The Royal Naval Reserve
20. The Royal Navy
21. Drum Horse and State Trumpeters of the Household Cavalry
22. First Detachment of the Household Cavalry
23. Two Bands of Her Majesty's Foot Guards
24. Four Chiefs of Staff
25. Insignia Bearers: Order and Decorations of the Deceased borne by four Officers of the Queen's Royal Irish Hussars
26. The Banners of the Cinque Ports and of Spencer-Churchill borne alternately by four Officers of the Queen's Royal Irish Hussars
27. Brigade-Major Household Brigade; A.D.C. to G.O.C. London District; Chief of Staff London District
29. The Earl Marshall The Duke of Norfolk
30. Royal Naval Gun Crew from H.M.S. "Excellent" with Bearer party from the Grenadier Guards
31. Royal Naval Gun Crew (Forward Detachment)
32. The Gun Carriage with on either side an Escort of The Royal Air Force

33. Royal Naval Gun Crew (Rear Detachment)
34. The Family and the Principal Mourners
35. Second Detachment Household Cavalry
36. Band of the Royal Artillery
37. Band of Metropolitan Police
Contingents of:
38. Police
39. Fire Services
40. 40.Civil defence Corps
41. Metropolitan Police Escort

It was an enormous assembly of personnel and stretched for a mile, half the distance from New Palace Yard to St. Paul's.

In New Palace Yard outside Westminster Hall the Guard of Honour was mounted by The Brigade of Guard Guards. The other Guards of Honour were the Royal Air

The naval gun carriage with its escort of Royal Navy officers and ratings leaves the Palace of Westminster.

Force in the forecourt of St. Paul's, the Royal Marines at Tower Hill, and the Royal Navy on Tower Wharf. Following the emergence of Churchill's coffin at 9.35 am carried by the bearer party provided by the 2nd Battalion Grenadier Guards, on that cold January day from Westminster Hall were the mourners consisting of close family members. As the coffin emerged, the order 'Off Caps' rang out and in perfectly synchronised unison the whole gun carriage crew doffed their white-topped naval caps. The coffin was placed on the naval gun carriage; the order 'On Caps' was called and the order to slow march was given by the Officer in Charge of the gun Carriage at 9.45am – at which time Big Ben struck the quarter to and was then silenced until after the funeral.

There were 10 R.A.F. personnel on either side of the Gun carriage with sloped arms. The gun carriage crew numbered four leading officers and 92 Ratings in the front detachment and two rear officers and 42 Ratings in the rear detachment. Behind the coffin marched four officers of the Queen's Royal Irish Hussars, each with a cushion carrying the insignia and medals Churchill had been awarded in his lifetime: The Order of Nepal, the Norway Order of St. Olaf, the Medals of Luxembourg, Belgium, Libya and Churchill's campaign medals.

The banners of the Spencer Churchill family and the Cinque Ports of which Churchill had been Lord Warden were also carried. The motto of the Spencer-Churchill's is *'Fiel pero desdichado'* which is Spanish, rather than Latin, for 'Faithful though unfortunate' and relates to Winston Spencer-Churchill, the father of the first Duke of Marlborough who was a Royalist during the English Civil War (1642-1651) and who was stripped of his status,

*The gun-carriage procession nears the
top of Whitehall, with Big Ben in the background.*

property and monies by Oliver Cromwell. Although following the Restoration, when King Charles II ascended the Throne, he was restored to his previous status and indeed knighted, he was never compensated for his losses. Hence his appropriate motto.

As the procession marched off, Sergeant Morehen in the control room of New Scotland Yard watching proceedings with his colleagues on piped television and images from other cameras noticed that whereas the front of the procession had moved off at the head, the tail had not. Consequently the procession became stretched causing some difficulties for the Queen to arrive at St. Paul's ahead of the cortège. Her Majesty arrived with just a few minutes to spare.

As the procession left New Palace Yard, Sir Laurence Olivier, who was part of ITV's commentary team read these words of Churchill which he spoke on his 80th birthday speech of thanks to the House of Commons on November 30th 1954. This was when Clement Atlee, Leader of the Labour party, presented Graham Sutherland's portrait of Churchill to him. Clementine hated the portrait so much, it was subsequently destroyed by fire:

> I am a child of the House of Commons having served there for 52 of the last 54 of this tumultuous and convulsive century. I have indeed seen all the ups and downs of fate and fortune there; but I have never ceased to love and honour the Mother of Parliaments, the model of the legislative assembly of so many lands. I have never accepted what so many kindly people said-namely that I inspired the nation. Their will was resolute and removeless and it proved unconquerable. It fell to me to express it and if I found the right words, you must remember that I have earned my living by my pen and by my tongue. It was the Nation and the Race dwelling all around the globe that had the lion's heart. I had the luck to be called upon to give the roar.

Half a million people lined the route of the procession from Westminster Yard to St. Paul's. Amongst them were representatives from many organisations with which Churchill had been involved during his life in peace and in wartime; contingents of the French and Polish WWII Resistance, the Danish underground who all flew in specially to be there on the day and who lowered their flags as the cortège passed. There was also a contingent of groundsmen from Churchill's school Harrow, together with Harrow Cadets.

The procession slowly advanced along Parliament Street into Whitehall then on through Charing Cross into the Strand past the churches of St. Mary Le Strand and St. Clement Danes and into Fleet Street, finally up Ludgate Hill to St. Paul's Cathedral. During its two mile journey, Churchill's body passed by buildings which had been significant both in his personal life and also in his long political career.

In Parliament Square stood St. Margaret's Church where in 1908, at the age of 33, he had married Clementine; one of the major events of the Edwardian social season in that year. Then in Whitehall past the various Ministries in which he had served; the Treasury where he had been Chancellor of The Exchequer from 1924 until 1929, on past the old Ministry of Munitions, where he had been pivotal in the development of the tank in World War One, then past the Home Office and the Colonial Office. Then past King Charles Street where are the underground Cabinet War Rooms which he used in World War Two and where so many momentous decisions had been made. Then Downing Street where he had served nine years as Prime Minister. On to The Cenotaph where on Armistice Day he had stood, sometimes in tears as the Last Post was sounded.

Then the cortège came up to The Admiralty from where he had commanded the Royal Navy in two world wars, the second appointment resulting in the famous phrase, 'Winston is back!'. Then on past Nelson's Column in Trafalgar Square and then past the statue of Gladstone – both of whom had also been granted State funerals. The cortège proceeded along Fleet Street, home of the British press at the time; the newspapers were always close to Churchill; he had worked as a reporter in Cuba in 1895 and then in the Boer War prior to his capture short imprisonment and stunning escape. They had praised and criticised him over his career almost in equal amounts but on this day their posters were edged in black in respect. On up Ludgate Hill and to St. Paul's where the Queen and the congregation would await.

During the procession from Westminster Hall to St. Paul's and thereafter from St. Paul's to Tower Pier there was a 90-gun salute, one fired every minute to represent each year of Churchill's life, fired from St. James' Park by The King's Troop Royal Horse Artillery.

The chief mourners who walked from Westminster Hall to St. Paul's behind the Naval Gun Carriage were, (with their relation to Churchill in brackets):

Mr. Randolph Churchill (son), Mr. Winston Churchill (grandson), Mr. Christopher Soames (son-in- law), Mr. Julian Sandys (grandson), Mr. Nicholas Soames (grandson), Mr. Piers Dixon (grandson in-law), Mr. Jeremy Soames (grandson), Major John Churchill (nephew), Mr. Peregrine Churchill (nephew) and Mr. Montague Browne, Churchill's Private Secretary.

Randolph Churchill, Winston's son had undergone a lung operation when part of his left lung was removed on March 10 1964. Winston, Randolph's son was concerned whether his father would be able to make the two-mile walk from Palace Yard in Westminster to St. Paul's, particularly up Ludgate Hill, some ten months after his operation, but he duly succeeded in his own inimitable and reverent style.

The Duke of Norfolk leads the gun-carriage procession as it continues on its way to St Paul's.

Her Majesty The Queen had allowed the other family mourners to use five of her carriages for the journey to St. Paul's. In the first carriage, the Queen's Town Coach, were Lady Churchill (wife), Lady Audley (daughter) and Mrs Soames (daughter).

In the second carriage were Mrs. Piers Dixon and The Honourable Celia Sandys (granddaughter), in the third, the 10th Duke of Marlborough and Lady Avon (niece). In the fourth were, Miss Arabella Churchill (granddaughter) and Mrs. John Churchill and in the fifth, Mrs. Peregrine Churchill, Miss Emma Soames (granddaughter), and Miss Charlotte Soames (granddaughter). Mary Soames recalled how very cold it was on the day and that they had a rug in their carriage but two

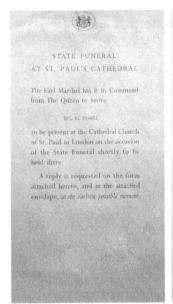 

The Earl Marshal's invitation to the State Funeral and (right) the cover of the document detailing the ceremonial arrangements.

officers came forward, to their surprise, with two small hot water bottles to warm their hands.

The bands in Procession played the following slow marches, with the drummers playing muffled drums:

    Dead March from Saul (Handel)
    Funeral March (Chopin)
    Funeral March No. 1 (Beethoven)
    Funeral March No. 2 (Beethoven)
    Funeral March No. 3 (Beethoven)
    Funeral March (Mendelssohn)
    Funeral March Regrets (Panne)

Song of Death (Sommer)
Vanished Army (Alford)

When the cortège reached St. Paul's there was a Guard of Honour provided by the Royal Air Force and on the steps of St. Paul's were members of the Horse Guards in their blue tunics and The Life Guards who, with their red tunics and the College of Arms Heralds, in their brightly coloured medieval tabards, added brightness to the otherwise very grey, bitterly cold January day.

At St Paul's, the bearer party was met by The Mayor of The City of London carrying The Mourning Sword covered in black velvet and the Ceremonial Pallbearers: The Earl Field Marshall Alexander of Tunis, The Earl Atlee, The Earl of Avon, The Lord Bridges, The Lord Ismay, Mr. Harold Macmillan, Admiral of the Fleet The Earl Mountbatten of Burma, The Baron Normanbrook, Marshall of the R.A.F. The Viscount Portal of Hungerford, Field Marshall The Viscount Slim, Field Marshall Sir Gerald Templar and Sir Robert Menzies.

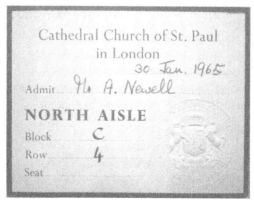

A seating card for the service in St Paul's Cathedral

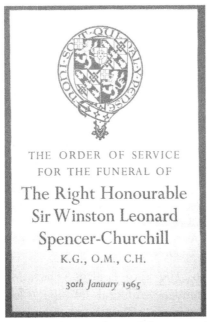

*Cover of the Order of Service for
those who attended at St Paul.s Cathedral*

Mountbatten commented during the 1950s, when the plans for 'Operation Hope Not' were being laid, that the ceremonial pallbearers on the provisional list were 'dying off like flies', but Churchill was surviving!

The English oak lead-lined coffin weighed three and a half to four hundred weights, a quarter of a ton, (392-448 lbs or 178-203 kgs.), which was an immense weight for the eight Grenadier Guards bearer party to carry up the steep and well-worn steps of St. Paul's. They had rehearsed this part on a dozen occasions, but on the second flight of steps a problem arose. The ceremonial pallbearers had walked down the steps from the cathedral to greet

Churchill's coffin at forecourt level to then escort it into St. Paul's. Earl Atlee, now a fragile 82-year-old and one of the ceremonial pallbearers, paused, returning up the second flight. The front bearers therefore had to hesitate and the weight of the coffin fell back on the bearers behind – particularly the last two, which caused an enormous strain, but the Grenadiers held fast.

There was therefore an understandable and wise pause by the bearer party at the top of the steps but then when they began to slow march down the aisle of the Nave they unfortunately set off, as all soldiers do with their left feet, instead of both sides remembering to step off with their inside foot followed by outside foot which ensures a coffin is carried in a straight line, which they had done carrying the coffin out of Westminster Hall on to the gun carriage and then from the gun carriage to the top of the steps of St. Paul's. This 'by the left' instinct resulted in the coffin going

The pallbearers ascend the steps of St Paul's Cathedral with Churchill's coffin.

down the aisle as Lieutenant Anthony Mather the officer in charge later put it, 'somewhat like a crab'. Nevertheless, Churchill's coffin was safely placed on the bier under the Dome, where it was cornered by four large candlesticks with their candles which had been last used at Wellington's funeral in St. Paul's in 1852.

Chapter 5

The Service in St Paul' Cathedral

The congregation numbered 3000, and the service was conducted in the presence of The Queen, Prince Philip, the Prince of Wales, (who had come down from Gordonstone, his school in Scotland) and leaders of over 100 countries including monarchs, Presidents, Prime Ministers and numerous other V.I.P.s. Nearly every reigning monarch of Europe attended. The ailing King Gustav of Sweden was represented by Prince Bertil. Also present were: President De Gaulle of France, the German Chancellor, and the Presidents and Prime Ministers of Canada, Australia, New Zealand, Israel, The Congo, Sweden, Japan, South Korea, and Malta, the island which had steadfastly held out during the dreadful siege in World War Two.

President Lyndon Johnson did not attend; he had been admitted to Bethesda Naval Hospital with an upper respiratory tract infection on January 23, the day before Churchill's death. He was represented by General and former President Dwight Eisenhower (who would later read a tribute on the BBC televised broadcast as Churchill was taken up the Thames to Waterloo), by Dean Rusk, Secretary of State and Earl Warren, the Chief Justice.

Those invited to the funeral had been sent an invitation from The Earl Marshall on behalf of The Queen, an Acceptance/Refusal form, a Seating Ticket and Car Label with route instructions and traffic instructions. They were also provided with a booklet of the Ceremonial to be observed at the funeral, containing complete details of the procession and with timings from when the doors of the cathedral were open at 8.45 am., and a booklet of The Order of Service. Both booklets were trimmed with purple borders.

THE ARRIVAL

At 10.00am the Dean and Chapter, who were accompanied by the Archbishop of Canterbury, the Most Reverend Michael Ramsay, the Bishop of London and the College of Minor Canons left the Dean's Aisle and went to the West Door of the Cathedral where they greeted the Speaker and then the Lord Chancellor. The Processions of the Lord Chancellor and the Speaker consisted of:

A Virger
A Doorkeeper
The Serjeant at Arms carrying the Mace The Speaker
The Trainbearer
The Speaker's Secretary with the Chaplain alongside a Virger
The Permanent Secretary to the Lord Chancellor
The Serjeant at Arms carrying the Mace

The Pursebearer
The Lord Chancellor
The Trainbearer
The Lord Chancellor's Private Secretary

Following these processions, the Heads of States with Royal representatives were received by the Dean and Chapter, as were Queen Elizabeth the Queen Mother and other members of the Royal Family, who were escorted to the Chapel of Saint Michael and Saint George. Then came the Lord Mayor and Sheriffs. At 10.35 am the Queen and the Duke of Edinburgh accompanied by the Prince of Wales arrived and were met at the foot of the steps of St. Paul's by the Lord Mayor carrying the mourning sword wrapped in black velvet. Having ascended the steps they were met at the West Door by the Dean and the Archbishop of Canterbury and then were escorted to the Chapel of Saint Michael and Saint George. The Queen's Procession consisted of:

A Virger
The Cross Bearer
The College of Minor Canons
A Virger
The Archbishop's Chaplain bearing the Cross of Canterbury
The Dean's Verger
The Clerk alongside the Registrar
The Bishop's Chaplain bearing the Crozier
The Lord Bishop of London supported by The Dean and The Lord Mayor bearing the mourning sword
The Duke of Edinburgh alongside The Queen

Queen Elizabeth The Queen Mother
The other Members of The Royal Family.

The Queen had graciously arrived before the members of the Churchill family in order that when they arrived after her, there was no protocol demanding that they should acknowledge Her Majesty by bowing or curtseying before they took their seats.

At 10.49am the coffin was carried into the Cathedral and placed on the bier under the Dome. The Procession was:

A Virger
The Sacrist
The Canon in Residence
The Persuivants of Arms
The Bearers of the Insignia and of the Banners
The Heralds with The Achievements
The King of Arms The Earl Marshall
The Ceremonial Pallbearers
The coffin borne by the Bearer Party
The family and other principal mourners

As the Procession proceeded down the Nave the choir sung 'The Sentences' beginning with the words from St. John's Gospel 11 verses 25, 26, 'I am the resurrection and the life, saith the Lord: he that believeth in me, though he were dead, yet shall he live: and whosoever liveth and Believeth in me shall never die.' Then followed the other Sentences from Job and Timothy. The music was composed by William Croft and Henry Purcell.

The service in St Paul's Cathedral, which was attended by members of the Royal Family, Churchill's family, and numerous heads of state.

On the right side of the coffin sat the family mourners and to their left The Queen and members of the Royal Family. In the front row of family mourners were: Lady Churchill, Mr. Randolph Churchill, Lady Audley, Mrs. Christopher Soames, Mr. Christopher Soames, Mr. Winston Churchill, Mrs Piers Dixon, Mr. Julian Sandys and The Honourable Celia Sandys. In the second row sat: Miss Arabella Churchill, Mr. Nicholas Soames, Lady Avon, The 10th Duke of Marlborough, Major John Churchill, Mrs. John Churchill, Mr. Peregrine Churchill, Mrs. Peregrine Churchill and Mr. Piers Dixon. In the third row were: Miss Emma Soames, Miss Charlotte Soames, Mr. Jeremy Soames and Mr. Montague Brown.

Churchill had wished for the service to have as its main theme Anglo-American unity and for there to be vigorous hymns, the latter wish previously conveyed to Anthony Eden. The first hymn was 'Who would true valour see' which ends each verse with 'To be a pilgrim', with words by John Bunyan and music by Vaughan Williams. Then followed the Bidding to Prayer by the Dean:

> Brethren we are assembled here, as representing the people of this land and of the British Commonwealth, to join in prayer on the occasion of the burial of a great man who has rendered memorable service to his country and to the cause of freedom. We shall think of him with thanksgiving that he was raised in our days of desperate need to be a leader and inspirer of the nation, for his dauntless resolution and untiring vigilance and for his example of courage and endurance. We shall commit his soul into the hands of God, the merciful Judge of all men and the giver of eternal life, praying the memory of his virtues and his achievements may remain as part of our national heritage, inspiring generations to come to emulate his magnanimity and patriotic devotion. And, since all men are subject to temptation and error, we pray that we, together with him, may be numbered among those whose sins are forgiven and have a place in the Kingdom of Heaven, to which may God by his grace bring us all.

Then the Dean read three prayers which were followed by the hymn, *Mine eyes have seen the glory of the coming of the Lord* – the Battle Hymn of the Republic written by Julia Howe with music by William Steffe, which emphasised the Anglo-American theme for the service. It was during the singing of this hymn that on this otherwise dark grey and bitterly cold January day, a shaft of bright sunlight shone down through the dome on to Churchill's coffin, which was such a poignant moment it caused shivers down spines. Then followed the Lesson, read by the Canon, 1st Book of Corinthians verses 15-20 which includes the words, 'O death, where is thy sting, ? O grave, where is thy victory?'.

The next hymn was also so appropriate; *Fight the good fight*, with words by John Monsell and music by William Boyd.

The Lord's Prayer was then said by the congregation led by the Minor Canon and The Collect was then read followed by the Choir singing, 'Give rest, O Christ, to thy servant with thy Saints: where sorrow and pain are no more; neither sighing but everlasting.' by Kieff Melody.

The Archbishop of Canterbury then read a prayer before reciting the Grace which was then followed by the singing of The National Anthem.

Finally, the 'Last Post' was sounded from the Whispering Gallery on a silver trumpet played by Corporal Wilson of the Horse Guards, followed by 'Reveille' from the West Window balcony by Sergeant Basil King of the Queen's Royal Irish Hussars who had come from his base in Germany for the occasion. As Sergeant King looked down he could see all the mourners seated around the bier and there also seated was his Commanding Officer which put him under even greater stress. When Sergeant King had finished 'Reveille', Richard Dimbleby who was narrating for the BBC televised broadcast and who was within sight, gave him a 'thumbs up'. Both renditions were note perfect and both haunting and heart rending. The trumpeters upon whom must have been incredible pressure given the moment of the occasion, were duly thanked and praised by their Commanding Officers and Directors of Music. During my interview with the Duke of Marlborough, he made particular reference to the impact that 'The Last Post' and 'Reveille' had upon him that day when he watched the service on television at Waterloo Station. As the echo of the trumpet's lasts notes faded away, Handel's Dead March was played on the organ.

(Details of the Service and Ceremonial to be Observed produced by kind permission of The National Archives, Kew).

As the coffin was carried down the aisle of the Nave, by correct step with its procession, the congregation sang the final hymn, 'O God, Our Help in Ages Past'. The Queen and other members of the Royal family, together with the Heads of State and Royal Representatives of the Heads of State, were escorted to the West Door by the Dean, the Archbishop of Canterbury, and the Bishop of London.

As the mourners emerged on the steps of St. Paul's the Bell Ringers of St. Paul's Cathedral Guild began ringing a 5007 Stedman Cinque which lasted 3 hours and 53 minutes. There were 12 bells rung by 13 ringers. The tenor bell weighing over 3 tons had two ringers who took turns to ring; the other bells weigh one and a half tons. The St. Paul's bells are the third heaviest Cathedral bells in the world. The bells were half muffled; a leather cover fits half way over the clapper, to achieve the muffled sound on one of its strikes. One of the Bell Ringers was Michael Moreton who although now 82 years of age still regularly rings at St. Paul's, but only on Sunday afternoons as he is busy ringing his local church bells on Sunday mornings!

The Queen and Prince Philip, with the Queen Mother and Prince Charles immediately behind them, and President Charles De Gaulle a few steps farther back, leave St Paul's Cathedral.

Amongst all the VIP.s standing on the steps of St. Paul's was President General De Gaulle standing tall, wearing his khaki greatcoat and distinctive khaki kepi with Queen Juliana of the Netherlands on his left and the Duke of Luxembourg on his right.

The Queen returned to Buckingham Palace, where she gave a lunch for members of the foreign royal families, presidents, prime ministers and other VIPs. (Churchill Archives Centre Ref: CHWL/ MSB. 325 Box 11). They included General Eisenhower; Dean Rusk, US Secretary of State; Chief Justice Earl Warren, representing President Lyndon Johnson; and His Excellency the US Ambassador.

Representing France were President De Gaulle; Admiral Cabanier; His Excellency the French Ambassador; and Monsieur Paul Reynaud, who was President of France in 1940 when France fell to the Germans. Reynaud was handed over to the Germans by Marshal Pétain, head of Vichy France, and was imprisoned until the end of the war in in 1945.

Chapter 6

The Procession to Tower Pier and on to Festival Pier and Waterloo

The gun carriage conveyed Churchill to Tower Hill via Cannon Street, Eastcheap and Great Tower Street, during which time the 90 gun salute by the Royal Horse Artillery from St. James' Park was completed. During the Gun Carriage procession to Tower Hill, Sir Robert Menzies the Prime Minister of Australia sitting in the Crypt of St. Paul's close to Neslon's and Wellington's tombs read on the BBC television broadcast, the following tribute, entitled, *One Fire Burning In Him*:

> As this historic procession goes through the streets of London to the Tower Pier, I have the honour of speaking to you from the crypt of St. Paul's Cathedral. I do this in two capacities. One is that I, Prime Minister of Australia, happen to be, in point of time, the senior Commonwealth Prime Minister and therefore speak on behalf of a remarkable world organisation which owes more than it can ever express to our departed leader, Sir Winston Churchill. He is one of the famous men whom we thank and praise.
>
> My second capacity is more personal and more

intimate. I am sure that you, most of you, have thought about Sir Winston Churchill a great deal and with warmth in your hearts and in your recollections. Some day, some year, there will be old men and women whose pride it will be to say: 'I lived in Churchill's time'. Some will be able to say: 'I knew him and talked with him and was his friend'.

This I can, with a mixture of pride and humility, say for myself. The memory of this moves me deeply now that he is dead, but is gloriously remembered by me as he goes to his burial amid the sorrow and pride and thanks, of all of you who stand and feel for yourselves and for so many millions.

Many of you will not need to be reminded, but some, the younger among you, the inheritors of his masterstrokes for freedom, may be glad to be told that your country and mine and all the free countries of the world, stood at the very gates of destiny in 1940 and 1941 when the Nazi tyranny threatened to engulf us and when there was no 'second front' except our own. This was the great crucial moment of modern history. What was at stake was not some theory of government but the whole and personal freedom of men and women and children. And the battle for them was a battle against great odds. That battle had to be won not only in the air and on the sea and in the field, but in the hearts and minds of ordinary people with a deep capacity for heroism. It was then that Winston Churchill was called, by Almighty God, as our faith makes us believe, to stand as our leader and our inspirer.

There were, in 1940, defeatists, who felt that prudence required submission or such terms as might be had. There were others who, while not accepting the inevitability of defeat, thought that victory was impossible. Winston Churchill scorned to fall into either category and he was right. With courage and matchless eloquence and human understanding, he inspired us and led us to victory.

In the whole of recorded modern history, this was, I believe, the one occasion when one man, with one soaring imagination, with one fire burning in him and with one unrivalled capacity for conveying it to others, won a crucial victory not only for the forces (for there were many heroes in those days) but for the very spirit of human freedom. And so, on this great day, we thank him and we thank God for him.

There are two other things I want to say to you, on a day which neither you nor I will ever willingly forget. One is that Winston Churchill was not an institution, but a man; a man of wit and chuckling humour and penetrating understanding, not a man who spoke to us as from mountain tops, but one who expressed the simple and enduring feelings of ordinary men and women. It was because he was a great Englishman that he was able to speak for the English people. It was because he was a great Commonwealth statesman that he was able to warm hearts and inspire courage right around the seven seas. It was because he was a great human being that, in our darkest days, he lit the lamps of hope at many firesides and released so many from the chains of despair. There has been nobody like him in our lifetimes. We must and do thank God for him and strive to be worthy of his example. The second thing I will never forget is this, Winston Churchill's wife is with us here in London; a great and gracious lady in her own right. Could I today send her your love and mine? She has suffered an irreparable personal loss. But she has proud and enduring memories. Happy memories, I venture to say. We share her sorrow, but I know that she would wish us to share with her those rich remembrances which the thought of the great man evokes.

There have been, in the course of recorded history, some men of power who have cast shadows across the world. Winston Churchill, on the contrary, was a fountain of light and hope.

As I end my talk to you from the crypt of St. Paul's, with its reminders of Nelson and Wellington, those marvellous defenders of long ago, the body of Winston Churchill goes in procession through the streets of London; *his* London, *our* London, this most historic city, this ancient home of freedom, this place through which, in the very devastation and fire of war, *his* voice rang with courage and defiance and hope and rugged confidence.

His body will be carried on the Thames, a river full of history. With one heart we all feel, with one mind we all acknowledge, that it will never have borne a more precious burden, or been enriched by more splendid memories.

(Reproduced by the very kind permission of Heather Henderson, the daughter of the late Sir Robert Menzies KT CH QC MP, Past Prime Minister of Australia, and also with the kind permission of The Menzies Memorial Foundation, Melbourne, Australia.)

In my correspondence with Mrs. Henderson she expressed her personal comments that she thought her father's address honouring Churchill was one of the finest speeches he had ever written.

I can still remember the profound effect Sir Robert's tribute had on our group of Selwynians watching Churchill's funeral on the BBC's televised broadcast in Trevelyan's old house on that January day in 1965. In the country pub 'Grasshopper on the Green' in Westerham, near Chartwell, there is a wonderful framed photograph showing Sir Robert Menzies and Clementine Churchill having unveiled a sculpture of Churchill, on the Green, donated by Marshall Tito and the people of Yugoslavia in 1969.

Churchill's coffin was then borne by the Grenadier bearer party to Tower Pier, a slow journey of 18 minutes. Half-way down the bearer party stopped for 15 seconds' rest, out of view of the television cameras. The Grenadier bearer party had defied a ruling that they should transfer Churchill's coffin to eight relief bearers halfway to Tower Pier. On the Friday rehearsal, the day before the funeral, they proved to their Company Sergeant Major they could carry the quarter-ton coffin all the way. The Guards had during the previous week arisen at 2 o' clock every morning for rehearsals and not gone to bed until 10p.m. They were so proud on the day that they had carried a coffin further than in any previous State funeral. Amazingly, Guardsman John Warner aged 26 had in the previous year fractured both his wrists and an arm on an assault course necessitating Plaster of Paris and a pin for months. His sister reported she did not understand how he had performed his duty.

From Tower Hill to Tower Wharf, the 60 massed pipers slow marched to 'My Home', 'The Highland Cradle Song', 'Mist Covered Mountains', and 'My Lodgings in the Cold Ground'. Having halted they played, 'The Flowers of the Forest', 'The Land of the Leal', and 'Lochaber No More'. The pipers came from the Scots Guards, the Royal Inniskilling Fusiliers, and the King's Own Scottish Borderers.

At Tower Wharf, the Royal Navy provided the Guard of Honour with the Band of The Royal Marines who played 'Sunset' and 'Tom Bowling'.

It was Churchill's wish that he had many bands and lots of music at his funeral and certainly his wish was granted. There were nine military bands who took part in the day's proceedings.

There was a 19-gun salute at Tower Pier fired from the

Tower of London battery by the 1st Regiment the Honourable Artillery Company, the first time in our history a commoner had had more than a 17-gun salute.

As Churchill was carried on to MV "Havengore", by the Grenadiers, he was piped aboard by the Royal Naval Piping Party. Their shrill notes cut through the quiet cold grey day and solemnity of the occasion. At her stern "Havengore" carried the flag of the Port of London Authority, the Blue Ensign with the half sealion, half dolphin holding a trident. In the bow stood the Bargemaster representing the Lightermen and Watermen of the River and the crew were members of the Port of London Authority.

MV "Havengore" was named after the Thames estuary island – a low lying marshy island off the coast of Essex. "Havengore" is derived from Old English; *haefen*, an anchorage, and *gor*, muddy, and is bordered by New England Creek, the River Roach, the Thames estuary and the North Sea. The launch was built by Tough Brothers, Teddington and is constructed of teak on an oak frame and was launched in 1956 and used by the Port of London Authority as a hydrographic survey vessel. Her motto is "Walk only in the ranks of Honour". She certainly kept to her motto on this cold January day. She is still berthed in St. Katharine's Dock and remains river worthy.

As "Havengore" cast off, the private funeral began and Mary Soames had a vivid recollection of Field Marshall Earl Alexander standing to attention and saluting on Tower Pier with his face contorted with grief as "Havengore" moved into the mainstream of the river.

The Duke of Marlborough during my interview particularly remembered the strains of "Rule Britannia" played by the Royal Marine Band as MVs "Havengore" and "Thame" cast off and motored upstream towards Festival Pier. The banks of the Thames were occupied by the thousands of onlookers who were quite silent in their respect, so the chief mourners felt they were all with them and they were not at all intrusive, very much in the tradition of the times in the 1960s, which dramatically changed with the noise and outpouring of grief for Princess Diana's funeral in 1997. But then Churchill had lived a full life and Diana had been denied so much of hers.

Aboard MV "Havengore" were: Lady Churchill, Mr. Randolph Churchill, Mrs. Christopher Soames, Mr. Christopher Soames, Mr. Winston Churchill, Mr. Julian Sandys, Mrs. Piers Dixon, The Honourable Celia Sandys, Mr. Nicholas Soames and Miss Arabella Churchill. The second launch, MV "Thame", also of the Port of London Authority, transferred the Earl of Avon, the Countess of Avon, the 10th Duke of Marlborough, Major John Churchill, Mrs. John Churchill, Mr. Peregrine Churchill, Mrs. Peregrine Churchill, Mr. Piers Dixon, Miss Emma Soames, Miss Charlotte Soames, Mr Jeremy Soames, and Mr. Montague Brown to Festival Pier.

"Havengore" and "Thame" were escorted by other launches of the Port of London Authority and Trinity House.

As "Havengore" motored up the Thames, on the BBC televised broadcast, General Dwight D. Eisenhower, past President of the United States, read this tribute to Winston Churchill:

> Upon the mighty Thames, a great avenue of history, move at this moment to their final resting place the mortal remains of Sir Winston Churchill. He was a great maker of history, but his work done, the record closed, we can almost hear him, with the poet, say:
>
> Sunset and evening star, And one clear call for me!
>
> Twilight and evening bell and after that the dark! And may there be no sadness of farewell,

When I embark.' (Alfred Lord Tennyson)

As I, like all other free men, pause to pay a personal tribute to the giant who now passes from among us, I have no charter to speak for my countrymen – only for myself. But, if in the memory, we journey back two decades, to the time when America and Britain stood shoulder to shoulder in global conflict against tyranny, then I can presume-with propriety, I think-to act as spokesman for the millions of Americans who served with me and their British comrades during three years of war in this sector of the earth.

To those men Winston Churchill was Britain-he was the embodiment of British defiance to threat, her courage in adversity, her calmness in danger, her moderation in success. Among the Allies his name was spoken with respect, admiration and affection. Although they loved to chuckle at his foibles, they knew he was a staunch friend. They felt his inspirational leadership. They counted him as a fighter in their ranks.

The loyalty that the fighting forces of many nations here serving gave to him during that war was no less strong, no less freely given, than he had, in such full measure, from his own countrymen.

An American, I was one of those Allies. During those dramatic months, I was privileged to meet, to talk, to plan and to work with him for common goals.

Out of that association an abiding-and to me precious-friendship was forged; it withstood the trial and frictions inescapable among men of strong convictions, living in an atmosphere of war.

The war ended, our friendship flowered in the later and more subtle tests imposed by international politics. Then, each of us, holding high official posts in his own nation, strove together so to concert the strength of our two peoples that liberty might be preserved among men and the security of the free world wholly sustained.

Through a career during which personal victories alternated with defeats, glittering praise with bitter criticism, intense public activity with periods of semi-retirement, Winston Churchill lived out his fourscore and ten years.

With no thought of the length of the time he might be permitted on earth, he was concerned only with the quality of the service he could render to his nation and to humanity. Though he had no fear of death, he coveted always the opportunity to continue that service.

At this moment, as our hearts stand at attention, we say our affectionate, though sad, goodbye to the leader to whom the entire body of free men owes so much.

In the coming years, many in countless words will strive to interpret the motives, describe the accomplishments and extol the virtues of Winston Churchill-soldier, statesman, and citizen that two great countries were proud to claim as their own. Among all things so written or spoken, there will ring out through the centuries one incontestable refrain: Here was a champion of freedom.

May God grant that we – and the generations who will remember him – heed the lesson he taught us: in his deeds, in his words, in his life.

May we carry on his work until no nation lies in captivity; no man is denied opportunity for fulfilment. And now, to you Sir Winston-my old friend – farewell!

(Reproduced by kind permission of the Director of the Dwight D. Eisenhower Presidential Library and Museum, Abilene, Kansas. (Ref: Sp-1 Tribute to Sir Winston Churchill 1/30/65, Box 8, Speech Series, Dwight D. Eisenhower: Post-Presidential papers.)

As "Havengore" passed Hay's Wharf, on the South Bank, all the cranes standing like a mustering of storks dipped their jibs in salute. Quite spontaneous; no one knew they were going to do it including the Metropolitan Police who at their monitoring centre at New Scotland Yard expressed some initial consternation but there was no need, as it was the loyal crane drivers' personal tribute to Churchill. There were 36 crane drivers involved who willingly had given up their time off on the Saturday without any resort to asking for overtime pay. Sir David Burnett, the managing director of the company, was proud his men had done this and arranged to have their expenses covered.

Then came what was expected and they did not disappoint: the flypast by the Royal Air Force Fighter Command consisting of 16 English Electric Lightnings of Squadrons 19 and 92 of R.A.F. Wattisham in Suffolk and from 56 and 111 Squadron from Leconsfield in Yorkshire led by Wing Commander A.F. Jenkins. The silver F1As, F2s and F2As flew over Tower Bridge and up the Thames at 500 feet and at a speed of 415 mph in four groups of four in diamond formation; their impressive 60 degree angle swept back wings were there for all to see together with their thin grey exhaust trails etching the grey January sky. The sound was amazing. The Lightning was an interceptor fighter designed to intercept Russian bombers during the Cold War. They were powered by Rolls-Royce Avon Turbo jets which could power the aircraft to Mach 1.7 and also to 36, 000 feet in shortly over three minutes. Pilots said to fly in a Lightning was like being strapped to a skyrocket. It was a great tribute to Churchill from the Royal Air Force. Their flight path from base took them over Colchester, Southend, Tilbury and then up the Thames, thereafter returning to their bases after an extremely successful and memorable mission.

As "Havengore" continues up the Thames from Tower Bridge, dock workers dip their cranes in salute and an RAF formation passes overhead.

"Havengore" and "Thame" on their river journey motored under London Bridge, Cannon Street, Southwark, Blackfriars and Waterloo bridges before arriving alongside at Festival Pier.

The arrival at Festival Pier coincided with the flood tide so the deck of "Havengore" was as level as possible with the jetty to facilitate the transfer of Churchill's coffin ashore. No doubt the timing of the flood tide was pivotal to all the timings of the day which may well have been back tracked from the time of the flood.

As Churchill was taken ashore, he was piped by the Royal Naval Piping Party.

The Grenadiers placed Churchill in a motor hearse for the short journey to the concourse of Waterloo Station. Their duties were now over. Lieutenant Mather subsequently said that they were all understandably physically and mentally drained. They returned to their barracks for lunch and a very well-earned 'very, very, large brandy'.

The hearse slowly drove from Festival Pier past the famous red lion at Waterloo station and on to the concourse where it was greeted by the new bearer party from the Queen's Royal Irish Hussars, an amalgamation of the 4th and 8th Queen's Own Hussars, the former being Churchill's first regiment when he entered the Army in 1895. As the hearse drove into the concourse, Richard Dimbleby read some words of Churchill:

> The day may dawn when fair play and love for one's fellow men and a respect for justice and freedom will enable tormented generations to march forth serene and triumphant from the hideous epoch in which we have to dwell meanwhile never flinch never weary never despair.

The Honourable Celia Sandys, in a television interview in 2014, made the poignant observation that the State funeral was where Churchill belonged to the nation and as Churchill's coffin was borne on to the funeral train, it was as though he was given back to his family, as a grandfather, a father and a husband.

The previous person to leave Waterloo after his State funeral was Earl Haig on February 3 1928, who was then taken to Edinburgh, again a most circuitous route, so perhaps the original State funeral nudge to the French. Haig's State funeral was at Westminster Abbey and the journey to King's Cross Station on the LNER line, the direct route to Edinburgh, was only just under three miles, but he chose Waterloo Station from where to leave. Although Haig respected the French as allies, he harboured a great distrust of them.

Churchill's coffin is taken aboard the funeral train that would travel from Waterloo Station to Hanborough.

Churchill's funeral train consisted of the Pacific steam locomotive Battle of Britain Class, "Winston Churchill", No. 34051, named in 1947 at Waterloo station by Lord Dowding, of Battle of Britain fame, and behind were six British Pullman Cars.

The 86-ton Pacific steam locomotive was designed by Oliver Bulleid, the Chief Mechanical Engineer of Southern Railways and had been built at their Brighton works in 1946. It had a 4-6-2 wheel configuration and in 1950 was painted into British Railways malachite green. The locomotive had been brought up from Salisbury to Nine Elms on January 25, five days prior to the funeral. Jim Lester the fireman on the locomotive wrote an interesting book entitled *Southern Region Engineman* in 2009, which contains a wonderful account of Churchill's funeral train. The driver was Alf Hurley, a veteran of Royal Train duties and fireman Jim Lester was just 22 years old; they had been selected after some previous visits by a footplate inspector on trains they were working. They suspected there was something afoot.

The locomotive with tender had a water capacity of 4,500 gallons (20,000 litres) and given the length of their journey and the stand-off time before and after departure, one of the prime considerations on the footplate was to conserve water as they would not be able to refill until the return from Hanborough to the Oxford depot. The reserve train in case of difficulties was another Battle of Britain Class, "Fighter Command", No 34064, which on the day was not required. This locomotive had also been named by Lord Dowding at the same ceremony in 1947 when he named "Winston Churchill".

Pullman takes its name from George Mortimer Pullman, an American who in 1864 built the Pioneer – the first railway carriage designed with true comfort for the passenger. The later creation of the Pullman Car Company in 1882 led to its domination in luxury train travel in the United States and later in Great Britain. Behind the locomotive was Pullman Brake Car No. 208, which was to carry the bearer party consisting of 10 Other Ranks, a Warrant Officer and Officer, then the Corridor Van (Bogie Luggage Van No. 52464) to carry the coffin. This van was built in 1931 and painted in Pullman colours in 1962 ready to carry Churchill and was kept out of public gaze in Stewarts Lane carriage sheds. When the empty train was shunted into Platform 11 at Waterloo it stopped where there was a distinctive white mark on the platform exactly where the middle of the doors of the bogie van should align.

There followed two Kitchen Parlour Cars, "Carinia" (1951) and "Lydia" (1928), which were to contain the main mourners numbering 20 to 25, then "Perseus", a Parlour

Car (originally ordered in 1938 but delayed because of the war and finally delivered in 1951), to carry the first party of 17 to 20 people. Last was the Guard Parlour Car "Isle of Thanet", to convey a maximum of 12 Railway Officers. (Churchill Archives Centre, Ref: WCHL 5/23).

The mourners, greeted on to the funeral train by the Marquis of Blandford, did not attend the service in St. Paul's but was at the interment in St. Martin's Churchyard as he 'wished to be next to his Father', the then Duke of Marlborough. He wore mourning dress not military uniform.

The bearer party carried Churchill's coffin up a short ramp into the bogie van and placed and secured it on the bier. They then placed Sarah Churchill's wreath of lilies and daffodils on her father's coffin, as although she had attended the service, having risen from her sick bed, she was not well enough to go to Bladon. (Churchill Archives Centre, Ref: CHWL/MSB 325 Box 11, p. 1363). Two of the bearers remained on guard in the bogie van during the duration of the 125 minute, 72-mile journey.

The television coverage by the BBC and ITV was watched by 350 million viewers around the world — then one tenth of the world's population. Richard Dimbleby, who gave a peerless and masterly narration, was paid £250 by the BBC for his services. The ITV commentator was Brian Connell, with Laurence Olivier reading extracts from Churchill's writings. There were 40 million European viewers, 12 million Russians, and 60 million American via Telstar 2, the communications satellite. There rapidly followed newsreels in colour by the Rank Organisation, shown in the West End the next day. British Movietone News and Pathe had already re-leased films of the Lying-in-State and both followed with films to be shown all over the world.

Whereas I, like many others, cannot remember exactly where I was when I heard of Churchill's death, due to the way the media had prepared us for ten days after his major stroke, for the inevitable sad news, I can, I suspect, like millions of others, remember precisely where I was when I watched the funeral on BBC Television. It was my last year at Selwyn College, Cambridge and I was living in the historian Trevelyan's house which Selwyn had acquired for student accommodation on the corner of West Road and Grange Road.

The Nunns were the housekeepers, Ted Nunn was also a Porter at The College and his wife kindly invited the student occupants of Trevelyan's old house into her lounge to watch the proceedings. It certainly was the most momentous event we had ever seen and there were times when there was not a dry eye in the house.

Shortly after Churchill's funeral train had pulled out of Platform 11 at Waterloo Station, Richard Dimbleby concluded the BBC transmission by reading the following:

From the Hall of Kings they bore him then, The greatest of all Englishmen,
To the Nation's the world's requiem
At Bladon.

Drop, English Earth, on him beneath,
To our sons and their sons bequeath His glories, and our pride and grief
At Bladon.

For lionheart that lies below,
That feared not toil, nor tears, nor foe, Let the oak stand, though tempests blow

> *At Baldon.*
>
> *So Churchill sleeps; yet surely wakes, Old warrior, where the morning breaks On sunlit uplands-but the heart aches*
> *At Bladon.*

Neither attribution nor title was given. The poem is entitled *Tribute* and was written by a teacher named Avril Anderson. She was born in Londonderry in 1908 and educated at Trinity College Dublin. She wrote poems, books and also children's plays, songs and operetta and taught Spanish.

On the off-chance she submitted her poem *Tribute* to the BBC and was delighted that it was chosen to be read by Richard Dimbleby at the conclusion of the BBC's televised coverage of Churchill's funeral. She died in 1988 aged 80 and is buried in the churchyard of St. Wilfrid's in Grappenhall in Cheshire. On her gravestone is inscribed the following from her poem *Tribute*:

> *'...yet surely wakes, where the morning breaks on sunlit uplands...'*

Chapter 7

The Train Journey from Waterloo to Hanborough

At 1.28pm, following a signal from the station master, the Royal Train Guard W.H. Horwill silently waved his green flag; there was an acknowledgement from the driver by a light touch on his whistle and "Winston Churchill", with its train of five Pullman cars, slowly and quietly steamed out of Platform 11, with a boiler steam pressure of 200lbs/sq inch, on its way to Hanborough some 72 miles and just over two hours away. On the front of the locomotive were three large white discs which had been transferred from the tender on arrival at Waterloo. The 'V' formation used, usually signalled a breakdown train, but on this occasion they had been placed there in memory of Churchill's famous hand sign, 'V' for Victory.

There was a four-page railway route plan produced which is now housed in the National Railway Museum Archives in York. The plan outlines the route with everything timed to the last minute, with instructions as to how and when communication should occur between stations and signal boxes when the train left, passed or arrived at key points along the route. It was signed off by S.D. Ward of Southern Region and H.M Lattimer of Western Region.

The train's route from Waterloo crossed the Thames at Richmond and when approaching St. Margaret's there was some concern on the footplate including the Chief Inspector Bill Neale as the distant signal for Twickenham was not raised despite obvious clearance for the journey. The signal was in fact defective which caused a temporary slowing of the train. Then on to Whitton and Feltham Junctions and Staines where the reserve locomotive "Fighter Command" was waiting in the wings in case of call-up. No traditional whistle exchanges were exchanged, just a friendly wave. Having crossed the Thames for the second time, the train speeded on to Egham, through Virginia Water and on to Chertsey. Shortly after Knowle East, the 22-year-old fireman, Jim Lester saw his proud parents standing on the railway embankment. Thereafter, the journey took them through Sunningdale, and on to Ascot, Bracknell and then arriving at Earley the beginning of the spur line connecting the Southern railway to the Western railway at 14.33hrs. The train stopped for two minutes between 14.34 and 14.36 hrs., and the Western Railway Pilot, Driver P. Talbot climbed aboard the footplate and the Western Guard H.F. Simmons also joined the train. Chief Inspector Neale insisted that driver Hurley continued to drive the train as although Western Railway drivers might be familiar with Southern Region trains they were not familiar with Pullman cars with their unique vacuum braking system which required some degree of proficiency. (Ref: *Southern Region*

The Battle of Britain class locomotive "Winston Churchill", pulling the funeral train containing Churchill's coffin, steams through the countryside towards Hanborough Station.

Engineman, p.72, Jim Lester, 2009, Noodle Books)

During the journey, drinks and lunch were served. The British Transport Hotels Ltd., Pullman Division issued written instructions on January 26 1965 regarding the catering and seating arrangements on the train. The main party were given lunch consisting of:

    Prawn Cocktail
    Chicken Supreme Panee au Beurre
    Asparagus Tips
    Green Garden Peas
    Peach Melba or Cheese Tray
    Coffee

The cost was 22/6d per head.

The instructions regarding drinks were as follows:

Bar Stock:
The standard stock cover is required. Requests have been made for wines and Champagne to be available and in good supply. Fruit juice and soft drinks also to be offered. The bearer party to have moderate supply.

The bearer party and railway officers had a plated cold lunch consisting of:

Ham and Tongue with Salad
Fruit Salad and Cream
Coffee

The cost was 13/6d. per head.

There were two chefs on the train together with seven Pullman Leading Attendants. Separate bills were to be issued to the bearers, railway officers and mourners. Account to be submitted to General Manager, Waterloo, ref:D.295.ST.

S.G. Johnson, who signed the instructions, concluded by writing, 'THIS SPECIAL BEARS AN IMMENSE AMOUNT OF WORLD WIDE PRESTIGE and will be seen at Waterloo by millions on Television. PLEASE GIVE THIS EVERY CARE AND SPECIAL ATTENTION.'

(Extracts taken from *Pullman Car Services Coupé News*, January 2005, No. 23 on the occasion of the 40th

Anniversary of Churchill's funeral train.)

Subsequent to the funeral, the 16th Duke of Norfolk told his great cricketing friend Alec Bedser that when the mourners boarded the train there were on a table bedecked with a starched white linen tablecloth, some bottles of Pol Roger, Churchill's favourite Champagne and leaning against them was an envelope addressed to the mourners. When opened there was a card with a hand written message from Churchill which read 'Don't be despondent, have a drink, Love Winston'.

When I asked the Duke of Marlborough, during my interview with him in his private study at Blenheim Palace, whether there was champagne on the funeral train from Waterloo he quipped ' of course there was champagne!'

'Pol Roger?' I enquired, to which the Duke retorted 'He never drank any other!' He also referred to Churchill's great friendship with Odette Pol Roger and he also knew of 'the Waterloo story' and De Gaulle.

Churchill first drank Pol Roger in 1908 and developed a close affinity with the House in 1944. At the conclusion of World War Two, Churchill attended a party at the British Embassy in Paris where he was introduced by the British Ambassador (1944-48) and his wife, Duff and Diana Cooper, to Odette Pol-Roger who had married into the Champagne family. She was one of the beauties of her generation and was one of three dazzling daughters of the French General Wallace who were known as 'The Wallace Collection'. From this meeting Churchill was to demand no other champagne.

Odette was a great anglophile and during the occupation of France in World War Two, Odette's garden in Epernay was always full of English flowers and she sported a brooch which she had been given, with the wings of the R.A.F. She was also a courier for the French Resistance.

Churchill and Odette formed a close friendship and subsequently Churchill became a high profile ambassador of Pol Roger. The American socialite Susan Mary Alsop said 'It was a beautiful December- May relationship, quite harmless and smiled upon by Mrs. Churchill, who much admired Odette'. (*Pol Roget & Cie., Epernay*, Cynthia Parzych and John Turner, CP Publishing 1999, p.138.)

Churchill would regularly receive a case of his favourite vintage 1928. When this vintage came to an end he drank the 1934 vintage until his death. He also arranged for Pol Roger to make pint-size bottles for his consumption as he felt a half bottle insufficient for his purposes and Lady Churchill felt a whole bottle was too much! Churchill once asked his close friend and scientific advisor Professor Lindeman how much space would be taken up by the champagne he had drunk in his life and Churchill was very unimpressed that it would have only occupied half a railway carriage!

Churchill even named one of his prize-winning horses "Pol Roger", which won the Black Prince Stakes at Kempton Park in the Coronation Meeting of 1953. When he sent Odette a copy of his signed biography he inscribed it 'Cuvee de Reserve, mise en bouteille au Chateau Chartwell.' Odette Pol Roger was invited to and attended Churchill's funeral service in St. Paul's. Following the death of Churchill, on Odette's instructions Pol Roger placed a black border around their bottle labels which were shipped to the UK in respect for Churchill's death. This was continued from 1965 until 1990, when the border was changed to dark blue, recalling Churchill's distinguished days at the Admiralty.

Now there is an even more fitting tribute in the form of the Sir Winston Churchill Cuvée, which is considered to be one of the greatest cuvées of the age.

During my interview with the Duke of Marlborough it was plain to see he had enormous respect and indeed great affection for Churchill, who was both his third cousin and godfather. The Duke related a memorable event in his life when he was 11 years old in 1937 when Churchill gave him a present of a gold watch. The Duke was then the Marquis of Blandford and Churchill had the watch inscribed with the words, 'To Blandford from Winston Churchill December 1937' and on the obverse, 'Remember John Churchill and William Cadogan'.

John Churchill was the first Duke of Marlborough who won the famous victory at The Battle of Blenheim and William Cadogan was his A.D.C. during the campaign. Cadogan was of enormous assistance to John Churchill and no doubt Winston Churchill had previously told his godson, the young Blandford, of their military exploits in the 18th century and perhaps also the fact that when Marlborough went into self- exile in France following alleged fraud during Queen Anne's reign, the very loyal Cadogan accompanied him before his triumphant return in 1714, three years later, at the beginning of George I's reign.

On the line from Waterloo to Hanborough, stations opened along the route so people could pay their respects as the train pulled through. The platforms were packed with people, the men removing their hats in respect. There were other touching sights of people and individuals paying their last respects: the single farmer with his dog standing to attention in a field, his cap in his hand; farmers with their children on ponies all standing quietly; the lock keeper standing to attention by his lock; the retired R.A..F Officer standing and saluting on the flat roof of his house in his old R.A.F. uniform. The 500 boys and staff of St. Edward's School in Oxford lined the railway at the bottom of School Fields as the train steamed past and some of the boys made their own mementos of the day by placing pennies on the line.

As the train approached Oxford, the driver had been instructed to slow down to 20 mph in order that the mourners would be able to hear the peals of bells from the bell towers of the city's spires which were clearly heard on the footplate of the locomotive.

Hanborough station, a small and somewhat dilapidated station where the German Kaiser had been when on a visit to Blenheim many years before had been smartened up with carefully placed linen drapes covering the tired and in many places flaking paintwork.

The exit road from Hanborough station is on the side of the up line i.e. the line returning to London. In order that Churchill's train stopped on this side of the station, switch points were placed further up the down line so the train switched over to the up line and therefore stopped nearer to the exit road from the station. It also ensured the carriages were on the up line for their return to London after the interment. Marker poles were placed either side of the track where the centre of the locomotive's footplate should precisely stop to enable the bearer party to alight with Churchill's coffin at the appropriate place on the platform.

It was written in the railway plan that the precise distance between the centre of the bogie van carrying Churchill's coffin and the centre of the locomotive footplate was 99 feet 5 inches. The train arrived at 3.23 pm. When the cortège left the train, "Winston Churchill" was uncoupled, transferred to the down line via the other switch points and returned tender first to Oxford depot, arriving with enough water to spare. Then came a treat for 22 year old fireman Jim Lester; the inspector asked him to drive the train back to Nine Elms in London, while the inspector acted as fireman and driver Alf Hurley sat back and enjoyed a good and well-earned mug of tea!

The hearse and funeral cars to take the cortège to St. Martin's Church and then return the mourners to the train for the return journey to London were provided by Elliston & Cavell Ltd., Oxford. The head of the company subsequently wrote to The Earl Marshall informing him that he would not be submitting an account; they considered it a great honour to have performed their duties for Churchill. (College of Arms Archives, Ref: Funeral of Sir Winston Churchill, Vol. VI, p. 310).

They were duly thanked by the Duke, as were Carters of Oxford, who assisted with the burial. Jerram's, undertakers from Woodstock, had attended to the grave, and Kenyons had overseen matters in London.

The short journey to St. Martin's church at Bladon was two miles. The roadsides were empty of people. Bladon was then a village of 400 people with two pubs. The village had been spruced up with buildings having been given a coat of paint. Outside one of the pubs, "The White Hart", six telephone boxes had been placed to accommodate the requirements of the world's press and tiny Bladon would thereafter have thousands of visitors a year who come to see St. Martin's and the graveyard where Churchill and his ancestors and family lie.

Chapter 8

The Interment at
St Martin's Church, Bladon

The coffin and bearer party were greeted by the Rector of St Martin's who was now The Reverend J. E. James, together with his son, who carried the Cross. No further service was held inside the Church. Churchill's coffin was therefore taken straight to the graveside where a short committal service was recited by the Rector. Albert Danby, the churchwarden stood by the vestry door with a chair at hand in case Lady Churchill needed it, but it was not required.

Here in the graveyard lay Churchill's ancestors including his father and mother and brother. Churchill's grave was dug by grave diggers from Jerram's, Father and Sons undertakers from Woodstock. In a radio interview after the funeral one of the gravediggers, Albert Jerram described in a wonderful Oxfordshire brogue how very very hard the ground for Churchill's grave was to dig with lots of rocks and felt it was very fitting for Churchill to be laid to rest there.

It is traditional in the churches of Western Christianity to bury a coffin with the head facing the East, just as church altars face eastwards, to be ready to rise at the second coming of The Lord. However the coffin, which was 6 feet 9 inches long was 1 foot 3 inches wide at both ends, but eighteen inches below the head end was 2 feet 3 inches wide (College of Arms Archives, Ref:Funeral of Sir Winston Churchill, Vol. IV p. 214) which was found to be too wide to be lowered into the grave which Albert Jerram and his mates had dug, with Churchill facing traditionally eastwards and so the coffin was therefore turned round where the grave was fortunately wider and was then gently lowered. So Churchill appropriately faces westwards towards his greatest ally the United States and to his mother Jennie's homeland. Peregrine Churchill, who was present at the interment, did say to Celia Lee some time after the funeral that he thought 'some wag' would eventually draw attention to the significance of this; it seems that responsibility has after 50 years, finally fallen to me. Churchill therefore rests head to head with his mother Jennie Churchill whose grave is immediately behind, with her facing eastwards. After the interment, Lady Churchill looked into the grave for a few minutes before leaving.

After the grave had been backfilled, the wreaths from Lady Churchill and The Queen were placed on the grave. These had been collected from Blenheim Palace by Special Constable Donald Thompson. Lady Churchill's flowers consisted of red roses and carnations and her card read, 'To my darling Winston, Clemmie'.

The Queen's wreath consisted of all white flowers; lilies, carnations and freesias with the message, written in her own hand:

The gravestone of Churchill, and of Clementine on her death in 1977, in St Martin's Church, Bladon.

'From the Nation and the Commonwealth in grateful remembrance, Elizabeth R'.

The only other wreath lying on top of the grave was one from Randolph Churchill and his daughter Arabella.

The other family flowers were banked around with one from the Honourable Celia Sandys with the message 'To my darling grandpappa, with fondest love, Celia'. There were others, spread out for yards either side; red carnations from Marshall Tito, yellow tulips from President Nasser of Egypt, a poppy wreath from the Queen's Royal Irish Hussars.(*Daily Mail*, Monday February 1, 1965 p. 2).

So there Churchill lies, surrounded by his parents and other members of his family in a simple English countryside graveyard along with commoners such as George Hunt, Eliza Dawes, and Thomas Long.

On the left hand wall of the porch at St. Martin's church is a blue painted wooden notice board with gold writing alluding to the peal of bells rung by the six bell ringers of St. Martin's after the interment on that January day in 1965. It was a peal of 5040 Plain Bob Minor rung over two hours and forty minutes with bells half-muffled and was conducted by Elliot Wigg.

The villagers had been requested not to line the road from Hanborough station to Bladon prior to the interment but when the mourners had left to return to the station, hundreds of people suddenly appeared out of nowhere and there were vast queues who quietly filed past Churchill's grave. Police had to hold crowds back while the grave was backfilled. By nightfall, 80,000 people had filed past. The crowds queued all night and the walk past lasted four days and nights and the fire brigade had to set up temporary lighting. Bladon, then a village of 400 people, was swamped; the police presence was in the high hundreds. A temporary car park only held a fraction of the cars that came, and the queues were over half-a-mile long and four deep, the people slowly walking up to the lych gate where the file narrowed to single file as it passed the grave, taking two and a half hours to go by.

To this day thousands of visitors from all around the world come to visit Churchill's grave and those of his ancestors. Local people wishing to visit graves of their loved ones need to visit the churchyard in the early morning or evening to avoid the crowds. On the Sunday, the day after the funeral, some of the villagers went to Woodstock for a memorial service. The Duke of

Marlborough was there with his son, the Marquis of Blandford and his wife the Marchioness. They went afterwards to the graveside and then in St. Martin's Church they sang *'O valiant hearts'*. But the 's' in hearts was dropped for the occasion so the verse was thus sung:

> O valiant heart, who to your glory came Through dust of conflict and through battle flame;
> Tranquil you lie, your knightly virtue proved, Your memory hallowed in the land you loved.

A villager commented that he thought that "they knew what they was doing when they picked that 'un." It seems he was speaking on behalf of the nation.

Also on the Sunday, Vincent Mulchrome reporting for the *Daily Mail* from Blenheim Palace in the room where Winston gave his first cry after his birth alluded to a single floral tribute, one of a minute posy of violets from two Herefordshire ladies who always sent flowers on Churchill's birthday. They stood in a glass by his first baby vest and by three thick red-gold ringlets cut from his head when he was aged five. With their posy, Mrs. and Miss Adams of Myrtle Cottages, Callow, Herefordshire sent a card with the legend, 'Life's race well run, life's work well done, heaven's crown well won, now comes rest.' One of Churchill's paintings of the lake at Blenheim was above the bed where he was born.

Chapter 9

Return to London

The return journey from Hanborough station in the Pullman carriages was pulled by the diesel locomotive "Western Champion", D1015, in its distinctive yellow ochre livery and front number of '1ZOO', which returned to London by the direct route to the Western Railway station Paddington, not Waterloo.

The driver was J.H.L. Brown, the second man L.G. Altrinngham, and the guard H.F. Simmons. The Headquarters Running Inspector W.A. Andress travelled with the crew in the cab. The locomotive had been made at the Swindon railway works in 1963 and was decommissioned at the end of 1976 having travelled 1,296,000 miles. Similar to the outward journey, there was a reserve locomotive standing by in case needed. This was D1028 "Western Hussar", also appropriately named, but was not required.

The train departed at 4.20pm and arrived at Paddington at 5.35pm. During the journey afternoon tea was served, consisting of:

> Egg or Tomato sandwiches Toasted Teacake or Toast
> White & Brown Bread and Butter Biscuits Cake
> Preserves
> Pot of Tea (Indian or China) The cost was 4/- per head.

The cost of hiring the Pullman Cars was 15 guineas per car. (*Pullman Car Services Coupé News*, January 2005 No. 23).

During the journey the Duke of Norfolk went up to Clementine Churchill and kissed her hand. On arrival at Paddington, she returned to her house in Hyde Park Gate. Clementine had dinner with her daughter, Mary, and her Private Secretary, Grace Hamblin. When Clementine finally retired for the night, as she reached her bedroom door, she leant over the balcony and said to her daughter lower down on the stairs, 'You know, Mary, it wasn't a funeral – it was a Triumph!'

And indeed it was a triumph for Churchill and his family and for all those involved in the amazing organisation of such a momentous day; the people who came to witness the day; and for the many millions who saw it on British television around the world. 'Operation Hope Not' under the leadership of the 16th Duke of Norfolk, Earl Marshal of England, was a magnum opus of immense proportion and moment – the likes of which we might never quite see again.

Conclusion

*'Don't be despondent,
have a drink, love Winston.'*

*David McFall's bronze statue of Sir Winston Churchill
at Salway Hill in his constituency of Woodford. It was unveiled in
October 1959 by Field Marshal Viscount Montgomery.*

Epilogue

On January 31 1965, the day after the funeral, Norfolk wrote a handwritten letter of thanks to Garter at The College of Arms. In it he stated, 'Bladon went very well, all peaceful and quiet. Very cold!!' The Duke then went abroad for a well-earned two week break. He received a letter of thanks for his amazing contribution to one of the most momentous days in our history from Her Majesty The Queen. (College of Arms Archives, Ref: The Funeral of Sir Winston Churchill, Vol. IV, p. 391-392).

The total cost of the funeral in the Civil Estimates of 1964-65 was £48,000 – which in 2014 would be the equivalent of £650,000.

The costs were itemised as:

Earl Marshall's Office £15,000
Ministry Of Defence £19,000 Travelling £2,000
Ministry of Public Buildings and Works £7,000
HM Stationery £3,000
Expenses HM Household £1,000
Other Expenses £1,000

(College of Arms Archives, Ref: Funeral of Sir Winston Churchill, Vol. VI, p. 308)

Following the funeral, a short report on the planning and the events of the day was provided by Lt. Colonel The Lord Freyburg, Grenadier Guards, who noted that when Churchill fractured his hip in 1962, eight commanders were informed to speed up the process of briefing for 'Operation Hope Not'. It was obviously thought that Churchill was not going to survive his injury and operation. The Lt. Colonel also alluded to the slower marching of the naval gun crew, also noting the shorter step of naval personnel compared with their British Army and Royal Air Force counterparts. He thought in future they should lengthen their step and increase their steps from 65-68-70 paces a minute. He also drew attention to the gap of 400 yards which developed between the Scots and Coldstream Guards in the middle of the procession due to a failure of the Scots Guards marshall to ensure this did not occur. Despite the criticism of the naval gun carriage party, he noticed the procession arrived at St. Paul's six minutes ahead of time at 10.39am – only four minutes after the Queen had arrived. Finally, he commented that the lead-lined coffin was too heavy – a sentiment that Lieutenant Mather and his bearer party would not have disagreed with.

(College of Arms Archives, Ref:Funeral of Sir Winston Churchill, Vol. VI, p.282,291).

Churchill was a colossus; he was a true Englishman, by birth English, and genetically English and American; he was made an honorary citizen of the United States by President Kennedy in 1963. Churchill was indeed a

Churchill in Honorary Royal Auxiliary Air Force Commodore uniform at Croydon on January 1st 1948 with cigar and V sign, there to open the new headquarters of 651 Squadron (County of Surrey) Royal Auxiliary Air Force. His R.A.F. uniform is on display at Chartwell.

Western champion who embodied man's will to resist tyranny. He was the linchpin of the Grand Alliance of 26 countries which overcame the Axis powers after six years of bloody war. Churchill was pivotal in the saving of Western democracy and the achievement of freedom from the tyranny of Nazi Germany. It is most appropriate that he now faces westward in the graveyard at Bladon in Oxfordshire. Churchill was voted the 'Greatest Briton' in the BBC television poll of 2002 and it bears witness and tribute to his greatness, that a huge number of those who voted for him, were not even born in his lifetime.

Churchill will be always remembered for his many qualities: his thirst for adventure, his leadership, his tenacity and courage, the power of his pen and his oratory, all with the essence of his British bulldog spirit with which he infected not only the British people but all those of the free world and which is surely echoed in his words from his world famous speeches to the House of Commons in 1940.

First, on May 10 – the day Churchill became Prime Minister – the conclusion of his speech was thus:

> I have nothing to offer but blood, toil, tears and sweat.
>
> We have before us an ordeal of the most grievous kind. We have before us many, many long months of struggle and suffering. You ask, what is our policy? I can say: it is to wage war, by sea, land and air, with all our might and with all the strength that God can give us; to wage war against a monstrous tyranny, never surpassed in the dark, lamentable catalogue of human crime. That is our policy. You ask, what is our aim? I can answer in one word: It is victory, victory at all costs, victory in spite of all terror, victory however long and hard the road may be; for without victory, there is no survival. Let that be realised; no survival for the British Empire, no survival for all the British Empire has stood for, no survival for the urge and impulse of the ages, that mankind will move forward towards its goal. But I take up my task with buoyancy and hope. I feel sure that our cause will not be suffered to fail among men. At this time I feel entitled to claim the aid of all, and say, 'Come then, let us go forward together with our united strength'.

Then perhaps Churchill's most famous speech of his life on June 10 1940, when he spoke thus:

We shall not flag, or fail. We shall go on to the end, we shall fight in France, we shall fight on the seas and oceans, we shall fight with growing confidence and growing strength in the air, we shall defend our island, whatever the cost may be, we shall fight on the beaches, we shall fight on the landing grounds, we shall fight in the fields and in the streets, we shall fight in the hills; we shall never surrender, and even if, which I do not for a moment believe, this island or a large part of it were subjugated and starving, then our empire beyond the seas, armed and guarded by the British Fleet, would carry on the struggle, until, in God's good time, the new world, with all its power and might, steps forth to the rescue and liberation of the old.

(Speeches and all Churchill quotations reproduced in the text by the very kind permission of Curtis Brown Ltd.)

We also shall never forget his great humanity. A man who could move armies, navies, air forces and peoples, yet could unashamedly be moved to tears when a poignant moment or scene came to his profound humane attention.

We certainly owe the freedom we still enjoy to this day to Churchill, to the men and women he led in the armed forces and in civilian and political life and to the example he set, the legacy he gave us, which thankfully we have enjoyed for 50 years since his death and which hopefully, we will continue to strive for its perpetuation of democratic freedom, for future generations to come.

Appendices

Appendix I

THE CHURCHILL FAMILY GRAVES AT ST. MARTIN'S CHURCH, BLADON, OXFORDSHIRE

Standing on the path in front of the grave where Winston Churchill and the ashes of his wife Clementine Churchill are buried and where Churchill faces westward, (towards you), the first grave on the right is that of Churchill's cousin, Ivor Charles Spencer Churchill.

Immediately behind Winston and Clementine Churchill's grave lies Churchill's mother Jennie Churchill facing eastwards. So Winston and Jennie Churchill lie head to head. On the right of Jennie Churchill's grave lies John Strange Spencer-Churchill, Winston's brother Jack. On the left of Jennie Churchill's grave lies Lord Randolph Henry Spencer-Churchill, Winston's father and to his left lies Randolph Frederick Spencer- Churchill, Winston Churchill's son.

Behind Jennie Churchill's grave lie three graves: the nearest is that of Diana Spencer-Churchill and then Sarah Spencer-Churchill, Winston's daughters and the farthest grave is that of Christopher Soames, Winston's son in law.

Turning to the left and beyond the end of the path on the left and surrounded by iron railings are two small graves, the graves of two of Randolph Churchill's siblings and Winston Churchill's uncles; Charles Ashley Spencer-Churchill 1856-1858 who died aged two years and Augustus Robert Spencer-Churchill 1858-1859 who died at the age of ten months. There was a third, Frederick John Winston Churchill 1846-1850 who died aged four and a half years but there is no record of his grave at Bladon.

Appendix II

SOURCES OF INFORMATION & BIBLIOGRAPHY

BOOKS

Churchill The Supreme Survivor, A.W. Beasley, 2013, Mercer Books.

Churchill: The Treasures of Winston Churchill, the Greatest Briton, Christopher Catherwood, 2012, Andre Deutsch.

The Wicked Wit of Winston Churchill, Dominique Enright, 2001, Michael O'Mara Books.

Churchill: A Life, Martin Gilbert, 1991, William Heinmann Ltd.

Finest Years: Churchill as a Warlord 1940-1945, Max Hastings, 2009, Harper Press.

The Bedsers Twinning Triumphs, Alan Hill, 2001, Mainstream Publishing.

Churchill's Last Years, Roy Howells, 1965, McKay.

Churchill, Ashley Jackson, 2011, Quercus.

Churchill, Roy Jenkins, 2001, Macmillan.

Winston & Jack: The Churchill Brothers, Celia and John Lee, 2007, Celia Lee.

The Churchills: A Family Portrait, Celia Lee and John Lee, 2010, Palgrave Macmillan.

Southern Region Engineman, James Lester, 2009, Noodle Books.
Churchill's Cigar, Stephen McGinty, 2007, Macmillan.
Churchill: The Struggle for Survival 1940/65, Lord Moran, 1966, Constable and Company.
The Last Lion, William Manchester and Paul Reid, 1983, 1988, 2012, Little Brown and Company.
With The M.C.C. in Australia 1962-3, A.G. Moyes and Tom Goodman, 1965, The Sportsmans Book Club.
Pol Roger and Co., Cynthia Parzych and John Turner, 1999, Cynthia Parzych Publishing Inc. and Pol Roger & Cie.
Man of The Century: Winston Churchill and His Legend since 1945, John Ramsden, 2002, Harper Collins.
Winston and Clementine: The Personal letters of the Churchills, Mary Soames (Editor), 1999, Boston: Houghton Mifflin.
Clementine Churchill , Mary Soames, Revised Edition 2002, Doubleday.

ARCHIVE PAPERS RESEARCHED AT ARUNDEL CASTLE ARCHIVES:

Funerals

Funeral of Sir Winston Churchill 1965
EM 3686 Letters numbered 1 to 303 relating to preparations in advance of,
EM 3687 and relating to, the funeral of Sir Winston Churchill. These letters are dated 20 Nov. 1958 to 31 Jan 1965.
EM 3688 A selection of letters removed from previous

group for special reasons. 1 file, 26 March 1959 to 16 Jan. 1961.

EM 3689 Papers relating to the organisation of the funeral; press conference; time-tables of ceremonial printed ceremonial and order of service. 16 items, Jan 1965.

EM 3690 Papers, inc maps dealing with the whole of the final arrangements for the funeral. 1 vol., Jan 1965.

Office of the Earl Marshall

DB103 Funeral of Sir Winston Churchill. Special District Order by G.O.C. vol., 1965 *(Operation Hope Not).*
DB27 Confidential
Report by the Manager M.C.C. Tour of Australia and New Zealand 1962/63
Arundel Castle Archive Papers Reviewed and referred to in the text by kind permission of His Grace The Duke of Norfolk

CHURCHILL ARCHIVES CENTRE, CHURCHILL COLLEGE CAMBRIDGE

Papers and documents researched:
CHUR 1/137 (162 folios) CHUR 1/138 (199 folios) CHUR 1/140
CHUR 1/141 (216 folios) CHUR 1/ 142 (92 folios) WCHL 5/3 (47 folios)
WCHL 5/14 Photograph of statue at Woodford Green, East London WCHL 5/23 British Rail Papers
WCHL 7 46 Books of Condolence from various British Embassies, High Commissions and Consulates including Turkey, Egypt, Laos, Peru, Cambodia, Morocco, Sierra

Leone, Japan, Serbia.
SEAG 2/4
CHWL/MSB 325 (Box 11)

COLLEGE OF ARMS ARCHIVES

Churchill Funeral Papers

Funeral of Sir Winston Churchill
Volume II General Correspondence 1957-59 Volume III General Correspondence 1963-1964
Volume IV General Correspondence 1965 Volume VI General correspondence 1960-1962
Volumes reviewed and referred to in the text by kind permission of Dr. Lynsey Darby Ph.D., Archivist, College of Arms, London

NATIONAL ARCHIVES, KEW

Papers and documents researched

ISS 39/21 CM8/209 CAB 21/5985 WO 32/20528 HO 342/109

Reviewed and referred to in the text by kind permission The National Archives, Kew, Richmond, Surrey

MAGAZINES, JOURNALS AND NEWSPAPERS RESEARCHED

London Illustrated News January 23 1965.
The Times January 25 1965.

New York Times January 25 1965.
Radio Times Supplement January 28 1965.
London Illustrated News January 30 1965.
Daily Mail February 1 1965.
LIFE Magazine February 5 1965.
London Illustrated News February 6 1965.
Paris Match February 6 1965.
Observer Supplement February 1965.
The Valiant Man (ITV Publication) 1965.
Finest Hour The Journal of Winston Churchill Winter 2012-2013 No. 157.
Model Rail No. 75 January 2005.
Steam World Issue 211 January 2005.

DIGITAL RECORDINGS RESEARCHED

BBC Audio Farewell to Winston, The moving Story of Winston Churchill's Funeral BBC Audiobooks Ltd., 2008 (CD).
BBC Archive video: The State Funeral of Sir Winston Churchill Parts 1-4
www.bbc.co.uk/archive/churchill/
11023.shtml, 11024.shtml, 11025.shtml, 11026.shtml.
The End of an Era The State Funeral of Sir Winston Churchill as televised in 1965 DVD Video GLDVD/ Y-03B Produced in association with ITN.

Appendix III

POEMS

Sarah Churchill

THE LAST FAREWELL

SC   We must brace ourselves to the fact That we may never meet again.
That the blood and tears that seal this pact Are not binding
When in later Years
This world we know has turned to lead Among the trebled billions of the dead We wander through pits of fallen stars Searching each other And Showing our hearts As token of our Love
To the sightless eye of space Let us now become aware That as in this moment
Of reality's sweet bliss All seems unreal and we Not really here;
So, in that blistering day of Truth, When among the lonely speechless stars
We wander – bereft of these dear scenes that we know – Unable to communicate –

we may yet... be there...

WSC   But where?

FORGIVE ME

Forgive me if I do not cry The day you die,
Streams at some seasons
Wind their way through country lanes of beauty And are dry.

The willow bends its head
To kiss the empty river bed With the same caress it gave
When on its heyday it was full and high Oh river know that I remember
The splashing laughter clatter Of a bubbling day in Spring
When everything was blossoming.

Butterflies still hover Down the rocky bed
And weeds grow strong and Guard the pebbled way.
In this high noon of nothing Which is death
Brave flags still wave
Cowslip-parsley, rag weed and sorrel Shout to me
That Spring is on her way Comfort, I am still to deaf to hear.

Yet forgive me if I do not cry The day you die
The simplest reason that I know You said you'd rather have it so
And that I held my head serenely high Remembering

the love and glory that we knew. Forgive me if I do not
   cry
The day you die... Forgive me
If I do...

(Both poems taken from *A Thread in the Tapestry* by Sarah Churchill, 1967, published by Andre Deustch and reproduced by kind permission of Curtis Brown Ltd, London.)

Sarah Churchill was the loving daughter of Winston Churchill. She attended Churchill's Funeral in St. Paul's having risen from her sick bed. She was not well enough to go to the interment at Bladon and her wreath of white lilies and daffodils was placed on her Father's coffin in the bogie van on the train to Hanborough. She died in 1982 aged 67 and is buried at Bladon.

OTHER POEMS:

Tribute, Avril Anderson, 1965. All reasonable attempts to trace the owner of the copyright have been made but have been unsuccessful.

Who goes Home, Cecil Day Lewis, 'The Room', 1965, The Complete Poems Stanford University Press 1996.

Churchill's Funeral: New and Collected Poems, Geoffrey Hill, 1994, Mariner Books, 2000.

Appendix IV

EVENTS COMMEMORATING THE 50th ANNIVERSARY OF CHURCHILL'S DEATH, HIS STATE AND PRIVATE FUNERAL

CHARTWELL, Mapleton Road, Westerham, Kent, TN16 1PS Exhibition, Death of a Hero, 15 November 2014 to 22 February 2015. Details at

www.nationaltrust.org.uk/chartwell

CHURCHILL COLLEGE, CAMBRIDGE:
Their statement reads:

"2015 marks the fiftieth anniversary of Sir Winston Churchill's passing. To find out more about his unique life and legacy and the events that are being planned to mark this commemoration. Visit

www.churchillcentral.com."

Acknowledgements

I owe an immense debt of gratitude to the authors Celia and John Lee, as without their support, advice, and great encouragement this book, without doubt, would never have been written. The email correspondence between myself and Celia during the past year and a half or so, has been in the legions. It was Celia who introduced me to Randolph Churchill and his wife Catherine and to Randolph's mother, Mrs. Minnie Churchill. My wife and I are so grateful to Randolph and Catherine Churchill for their most warm hospitality in December 2013, when they entertained us at their house in Crockham and when Randolph shared with us some wonderful stories of his great grandfather and showed us some wonderful Churchill heirlooms including the wonderful Low cartoon of Churchill when an in-patient at The Middlesex Hospital, London, after fracturing his hip in 1962.

I hugely appreciate Randolph's great personal support for me writing this book. I am so grateful to Mrs. Minnie Churchill for reliving her memories of the Lying-in-State in Westminster Hall and her hospitalisation in Westminster Hospital at that time, having just given birth to Randolph two days before Churchill's death. It was Celia who facilitated my meetings with the 11th Duke of Marlborough at Blenheim and the Countess of Avon in London. I am much indebted to John Forster, the Archivist at Blenheim and also the Duke's secretary Caroline McCormack for making the arrangements for my interview with the Duke of Marlborough in January 2014 and to His Grace for allowing me to meet him in his Private Study when he shared his memories of Winston Churchill's funeral and events surrounding it together with very happy memories of Churchill as the Duke's third cousin and godfather.

I am most grateful to the Countess of Avon (who attended the funeral) for sharing with me during our meeting in her London apartment in December 2013 memories of the close political relationship between her husband, Anthony Eden, and Churchill. I also wish to acknowledge the wonderful support for my project from Allen Packwood, the Director of the Churchill Archives Centre at Churchill College, Cambridge and Katherine Barnett, the House and Collections Manager and all her enthusiastic staff at Chartwell, together with Lee Pollock, the Director of *Finest Hour* – the quarterly publication of The Churchill Centre.

I am grateful to David Freeman, Editor of Publications, The Churchill Centre at the Department of History, California State University in Fullerton, for his advice and support. Also thanks to Randolph Churchill for putting me into contact with David Morehen, who was a police sergeant at New Scotland Yard, the headquarters of the Metropolitan Police in London, on the day of Churchill's funeral. I would like to particularly thank David for relaying his memories of the event and everything leading up to it, together with his involvement with the arrangements and for his kind loan of the police plans for the funeral.

In the order in which I researched the archives visited, I wish to sincerely thank the staff at the Arundel Castle Archives, West Sussex: Heather Warne, who was archivist when I visited the archives in 2013, and her assistant, Margaret Richards, and now Rebecca Hughes, the archivist who has been so very helpful. Also special thanks to Craig Irving, now Assistant Archivist whose feats of athleticism running up and down the turret stairs to retrieve requested documents was most impressive. Then to The Churchill Archives Centre at Churchill College Cambridge; particular thanks to Allen Packwood, the Director; to Julie Sanderson the Archives Administrator; and to all the staff who were so very helpful in my research.

I am especially grateful to Curtis Brown Ltd., to Gordon Wise, Manager, and to Richard Pike and Kealey Rigden for all their kind assistance and for their most generous permission to quote widely from Churchill's written and spoken words and also their very kind permission to quote two poems by Sarah Churchill at the end of the book. Many thanks also to the staff of the National Archives at Kew including Mark Dunton, Principal Record Specialist, and Judy Noakes, an information policy adviser there, and all their colleagues.

I am most grateful to Dr. Lindsey Darby Ph.D., the Archivist at the College of Arms for all her help with the many Churchill volumes archived there which she very kindly provided for me on my visit and for all her subsequent advice and guidance.

I wish to acknowledge the help, advice and encouragement of my great friend Dr. Pola Rosen D.Ed., Editor of

Education Update in New York City, whose enthusiasm for my publication together with advice on what would particularly interest American readers was so very instructive and greatly appreciated.

There are many others to whom I am indebted: Pamela Shearman, Office Manager, The Menzies Foundation in Melbourne Australia, who kindly contacted Mrs. Heather Henderson, the daughter of the late Sir Robert Menzies, the President of Australia at the time of Churchill's death and who, with The Menzies Foundation, so very kindly gave me permission to reproduce her father's tribute to Churchill transmitted by the BBC from the Crypt of St. Paul's after the funeral service. Also Valoise Armstrong, Archivist at the Dwight D. Eisenhower Presidential Library and Museum, Abilene, Kansas for kindly obtaining permission from the Director to allow me to reproduce the tribute given by General Eisenhower to Churchill as his body was borne down the Thames to Festival Pier and which was transmitted in the BBC television broadcast; and Dr. John H. Mather, a fellow Middlesex Hospital London, student and doctor, whose extensive knowledge of Churchill's medical history was so very helpful in my research; I am so very grateful to him for sharing all his knowledge with me.

The Reverend Jane Proudfoot Rector of St. Wilfrid's and her Churchwarden for their information regarding Avril Anderson, who wrote the poem in tribute to Churchill and who with her husband now lie buried in St. Wilfrid's churchyard in Grapenhall, in Cheshire. Canon Adrian Daffern, Team Rector for the Benefice of Blenheim who gave me information about the graveyard and church of St. Martin's, Bladon. George Webster a member of the Earl Haig foundation who afforded me information regarding

Earl Haig's funeral also leaving from Waterloo for Edinburgh. Jim Lester the fireman on the locomotive "Winston Churchill", which pulled Churchill's train to Hanborough for Bladon in Oxfordshire and who kindly afforded me access to a copy of his book, *Southern Railwayman*, within which is an account of Winston Churchill's funeral train. Angela Nicholls who as a nurse to Churchill in the 1960s gave wonderful insight during my interview with her in 2014, into her experiences of being a member of a team caring for him and David Bassford, Secretary of the Guild of Ringers, St. Paul's for putting me into contact with Michael Morton, now in his 80's and who was a bell ringer at St. Paul's when the peal was rung as Churchill's cortege proceeded from the Cathedral down to Tower Hill after the funeral service.

I would particularly like to thank Mark Dowd of Topfoto for all his help with obtaining photographs of Churchill's funeral, together with Lucy Kelly of Getty Images, who kindly helped with the splendid cover photograph. I would wish of course to thank my son, Alex Croft for designing the book's cover and also my son, Alistair, for his advice regarding legal aspects. Thanks also to Sophia Brothers, Image Executive, Science and Picture Library at the Science Museum in London who provided the photograph of the funeral train steaming its way into Hanborough and Kristy Heyman, Search Engine Assistant at the National Railway Museum, York, for providing a copy of the detailed railway plan for the journey from Waterloo to Hanborough.

I am of course, forever most grateful, that I had as great friends for over 35 years, the cricketing Bedser twins, Sir Alec and brother Eric and to Alec for telling me the stories regarding Churchill's funeral as told to him by the 16th Duke of Norfolk, without which this book would never have been born. I am also grateful to my late Mother who decided to give birth to me six weeks prematurely, which with her annual reminder on my birthdays forged a great affinity for Churchill who had experienced a similar neonatal experience to myself. It turned out Richard Langworth editor of *Finest Hour* actually did me a huge favour, as by rejecting my letter outlining Norfolk's stories about Churchill's funeral, as they could not be corroborated, providing the trigger point that spurred me ever on to carry out all my research resulting in this book.

More recently, I would like to thank Katherine Barnett, the House and Collections Manager at Chartwell, for giving my wife and I a wonderful private tour there, which gave us further insight into Winston Churchill and his wife Clementine, and for introducing us to a very special cat, Jock VI. Her support for my book, to be referred to in the forthcoming exhibition at Chartwell, Death of a Hero, commemorating Churchill's death is hugely appreciated.

I wish particularly to thank John Ransley of eBook Versions – whose advice, help, and patience regarding formatting my manuscript for self-publication of this book and its associated ebook editions, and all that goes with it, was outstanding. I certainly could not have done this without him.

I now go full circle and return to Celia and John Lee; Celia who most kindly proof read my manuscript and John who was Copy Editor, whose skills are hugely appreciated; eternal thanks to them both again. I owe an enormous debt of gratitude to Andrew Roberts, the famous historian and great Churchillian expert, who did me the enormous honour of writing his most kind Foreword. I am extremely grateful to him.

Finally, as always, my heartfelt thanks to my dear wife, Hazel-Ann, whose encouragement, always constructive criticism and patience are, as ever, hugely appreciated. And to my daughter Antonia for her ever-effervescent support of yet another 'Daddy project'.

To this highly impressive team who have assisted me in this venture go my heartfelt and everlasting thanks.

About the author

Rodney J Croft is now a semi-retired general and vascular surgeon in London, having retired from the National Health Service in 2004. He is Dean of Clinical Studies U.K. for St. George's University School of Medicine, Grenada, West Indies. The school has 17 N.H.S. Affiliated hospitals in the UK which are used for the clinical training of St. George's students. Since 1979 when the clinical programme began, more than 12,000 graduates from over 140 countries world wide have been trained in U.S. and U.K. affiliated hospitals. Many of whom now practice in countries of the Commonwealth and in the United States and Canada.

A Lancastrian by birth, he attended Bolton School in Lancashire and was thereafter educated at Selwyn College

Cambridge where he read medicine and then The Middlesex Hospital Medical School in London, qualifying in 1968. He was President of the Cambridge University Medical Society(1964-1965). He gained his Fellowship of the Royal College of Surgeons England in 1972 and was awarded his Master of Surgery degree at Cambridge University in 1982. In 1984 he became a Fellow of the American College of Surgeons. He was made a Liveryman of The Worshipful Society of Apothecaries in 1980 and became a Freeman of the City of London in 1982.

He began his association with St.George's University School of Medicine in 1980 when he began teaching students at The North Middlesex University Hospital. During his time at North Middlesex he was the Director of Medical Education (1986-2001), was made Professor of Surgery in 1999 and was appointed Chairman of the UK Surgical Faculty (2000-2003). He was appointed Dean of Clinical Studies UK in 2003.

During his appointment at North Middlesex University Hospital, he also gained wide experience of UK medical undergraduate teaching. He served as Clinical Sub-Dean at The Royal Free Hospital Medical School; latterly, The Royal Free University College Medical School for thirteen years and was a member of the Governing School Council for nine years. He was awarded the School Medal of The Royal Free in 1993. He was appointed Honorary Senior Lecturer in Surgery at London University in 1994, and was an examiner in Final MB BS (1989-2004).

Since 1986 he has been involved with writing major standards for cardiovascular Implants, initially representing the British Standards Institute,(BSI), then CEN, the European Standards Organisation and also ISO, the International Standardization Organisation. He has been the principal UK Expert for cardiovascular implants since 1993.

Publications include his contribution to a number of major cardiovascular standards as well as many scientific articles on general and vascular surgical topics. He is a Fellow of a number of professional societies. He was commissioned as a Captain in the Royal Army Medical Corps TAVR (1972-1974) and thereafter as Surgeon Lieutenant Commander, Royal Naval Reserve (1974-1983). He has travelled widely both professionally and for pleasure. He lives on the outskirts of London near Churchill's old constituency, Woodford; and is married with three grown-up children.

His recreations include travel and music – classical, opera, choral and jazz. He is a keen clarinet and saxophone player and, when time permits, he loves cycling in his beloved Epping Forest.

Rodney J Croft is a member of the M.C.C., The Garrick Club, and The Lord's Taverners. The Final Farewell: The State and Private Funeral of Sir Winston Churchill is his first historical publication.

Made in the USA
Coppell, TX
02 December 2020

42751448R00095